Praise

M000206309

"*Sliding Home* is a beautifully v .... Suz Ross first asked me if I would read it, she said that it centered around the year that she and her husband Jeff homeschooled their sons Matt and Tim. While that is true, this book travels far beyond a description of home-schooling. With impressive insight, humility, and honesty, Suz shares her thoughts and emotions as a mother, wife, daughter, educator, and friend. Her book reads like a novel as she describes the many people and events in her life, all of whom come alive in a vivid fashion. Her book also highlights her son Tim's struggles with reading and captures the importance of identifying and reinforcing what I call each child's 'islands of competence' to ignite their passions and love of learning. I believe that *Sliding Home* will be read and re-read and each time the reader will gain new appreciation of Suz's wisdom and her belief in the resilience of both children and adults."

– Robert Brooks, Ph.D., Faculty (part-time), Harvard Medical School. Co-author, *Raising Resilient Children* and *The Power of Resilience: Achieving Balance, Confidence, and Personal Strength in Your Life*

"Soulful, honest, engaging, rich with detail and warmth, wise, and in-structive... *Sliding Home* offers a balanced consideration of the pros and cons of public, private, and homeschool education. Ross is a gifted writer and educator, and it is a true pleasure to follow along with her on her family's adventures. She arrives at many core insights about life, learning, and parenting which are demonstrated beautifully through a graceful and inspiring story arc. It's fabulous!"

— Karen Merriam, M.Ed., Homeschool Teacher and Advisor

Sliding Home

Two Teachers Head to the Mountains to Teach Our Kids for a Year

Susan Cole Ross

Published by Piscataqua Press
an imprint of RiverRun Bookstore
32 Daniel Street
Portsmouth NH 03801

ISBN: 978-1-950381-70-8

Every moment and every word of
this story has been for our boys:

Matthew Brooks Ross

&

Timothy Wilson Ross

And was co-created with my patient
and dedicated husband, Jeff.

Author's Note

When Tim, somewhat impatiently, asked me why I hadn't published *Sliding Home* yet, I told him how I was concerned that telling our story might exploit him and his learning disability. "That's stupid, Mom," he protested, wise beyond his years. "It might show other parents how to help their kids deal with learning disabilities!" I didn't tell him that I was also just shy about it, about exposing our intimate family life, inextricable from their schooling that year, and I worried about Matt's privacy too. A tender young teen, he was becoming so much like his dad – a sweet, solemn, bashful, baseball guy with an unquenchable thirst for knowledge. Indeed, while I wrote, Matt suggested, "Couldn't you fictionalize it, Mom?" However later, recognizing the value of a primary source, he understood why, in the interest of authenticity, I did little to edit my journal beyond changing our friends' names. So, suddenly, when I finally felt ready to send it out into the world, he, a college freshman, edited the manuscript and wrote its introduction. Either he had come to like the idea of our story being published, or at least he wanted the opportunity to put his own spin on it!

Preface:

Looking Back on our Year of Homeschooling
from the Learning Specialist's Perspective

AUGUST 2020

Well, it took a pandemic and a country full of parents schooling their children at home, for me to finally screw up the courage and make the time to share my journal, *Sliding Home*. While our story certainly explores some good homeschooling choices my family made that year, it is more an exploration of the exquisite value of taking a year to step off the ride and be a family working together, recreating together, and helping each other learn and grow. In the chronicle that follows, readers can share how we created learning moments and continued our children's educations on a uniquely individualized level, while still working part-time, exploring nature and America, and creating a family life none of us had previously imagined. Rereading the manuscript, I see that all four of us became teachers and learners that year. In so doing, Jeff and I did less formal teaching than anticipated and more sharing: how we learn, how we explore the world, and how we develop new interests and talents in ourselves. We taught our kids less about academics, though we fit that into every morning, and more about self-motivation, resilience, and how to become the healthy people they want to be. We modeled adulthood, and we met the delightful adults our sons would become.

There are moments here when I am struck by our extraordinary privilege to be sure. We had enough money to get by on a tight budget and Jeff's sabbatical income for the year. We had an affordable family health care plan. We had parents who had already gifted us with strong educations. We had friends and family who provided connections that made the year a rich and rewarding experience. And we had a place to go that offered a new way of life to explore every day with relative ease. That place, aptly named the White Mountains for the color of its mountains but also aptly describing the color of the majority of its population, was an easy fit for us. However, I am acutely aware that relocating to a predominantly white neighborhood might not be as easy for our black neighbors and friends from Hartford County. We were fortunate but still daunted.

I am equally struck by our challenges. One of us had to quit their job, and we had no real savings to fall back on. We had to pack up our entire home into one room and take only necessities, mostly school supplies. We had no internet, in part because it was so expensive and in part because it was so new. Indeed, with it, the purely academic part of each day would have been right at hand, as would a myriad of museums, a world of experts and a bevy of books. Ours was another kind of remote learning. That is also what made it so special. With so much schooling happening online these days, children may benefit at home from more of the unplugged learning that we delved into. Our opportunities to learn away from the computer strike me as uniquely precious and prescient.

Our distinct privileges and challenges aside, and two and a half decades past, I suspect this book has more relevance today than ever.

It serves not as a how to reference, nor as a perfect paradigm for homeschooling. Rather, I hope that it shows that there is no formula and shouldn't be, because each learner and each family is different and their diversity offers the greatest potential for authentic and meaningful learning. Schooling at home is more art than science and resembles tutoring and modeling far more than teaching a classroom full of students. In illustrating how our family uniquely crafted a learning community to fit each of us, every opportunity and every season, I hope that other families feel invited and inspired to craft their own. Ours is just a story. A story whose time has finally come.

A grandmother now, I greatly credit my children and husband for helping me to have since become a professional in the field of learning and motivation. Looking back at our sabbatical after twenty-five years of parenting and instructing teachers on educational methods and incentives, I believe this journal shares, on a personal level, critical reflections on the essence of teaching and learning. Piaget documented much of what we know about how children learn by observing his own children at home. In the same tradition, Jeff and I observed, taught, and coached our preteen sons to levels of success we did not dream to expect. At its best moments, our story illuminates how children quench their natural curiosities. It explores how they find what my friend and colleague Dr. Robert Brooks calls their "islands of competence," those areas where a child shines and finds out how to contribute his talents and passions to the world. Today, I hope this story may empower families to explore such possibilities in the face of extraordinary times. Together, I hope we can make this a time of extraordinary possibilities for our children.

Introduction

Looking Back on our Year of Homeschooling
from the Student's Perspective

By Matthew Brooks Ross, 19 years

January 2002

My family decided to go on sabbatical during my eighth grade year. Aside from the fact that it would separate me from my best friend, Kelly, completely for a year and by a grade level thereafter, I was excited about the idea. At the time, I felt that my life lacked adventure. Windsor, Connecticut had been my hometown for ten years, and I desperately wanted to experience something new. I suppose the rest of my family felt the same way. It wasn't that we were dissatisfied with our current lifestyle; our suburban home was comfortable, but we all needed a change of pace. A year away from our daily routines offered the perfect remedy. The next question, of course, was where. We tossed around thoughts of going to Europe or Australia, but we all felt that such an excursion would be too extreme. Eventually, our sights settled on New Hampshire, my mother's childhood home and our family's vacation state. When friends of the family offered us a place to stay and a school for my father to coach at part-time, we were sold. Things happen for a reason.

I loved our year. We found all of the adventures I had been searching for. The woods of New Hampshire offered me hours of enjoyment that I had previously found only on television, and I found a new friend in my younger brother. The first months sequestered on a lonely, but beautiful hilltop forced us to bond as we had never had to in Connecticut. We camped out, blazed trails, built fires, and fought mini-wars with our dime-store disc guns. While our homeschooling did not follow a strict or terribly rigorous path, it offered me a new look at education. I began choosing my own books, my own research projects, and my own experiments. I was afforded the freedom I desperately needed to learn to love learning. Neither Tim nor I planned to progress a grade. My fall birthday had left me a young eighth-grader who needed another year to mature physically and intellectually, while Tim's dyslexia had left him behind his grade level in critical skills, especially reading. I did enough structured mathematics, French, and vocabulary development to refresh my summer-erased memory and deepen my understanding of these topics, but my real education came with my freedom to explore areas of special interest to me such as the Vietnam War, travel and the writings of Michael Crichton. My family's real education came with our freedom to explore life in the country and new vistas across America. We learned together.

When the year was up, I was happy to get back home. My appetite for adventure and change satisfied, I eagerly returned to my old life. I was also extremely excited to be entering Loomis Chaffee as a freshman. The college preparatory school had always been my home, and now it became my school. I became one of the "big kids" I idolized as a child. I returned with a rested soul and an eager mind, ready for high school. Tim also gladly returned to the life he had left behind. With his reading ability up to grade level and his newfound confidence in school, he was ready to become a serious sixth grader at Watkinson School. We both returned to the lives that had become stale to us with new energy, excitement, and appreciation.

Tim struggled off and on through his first four years at Watkinson, but rather than retreat into his helpless hole of "I'm stupid," he rose to the challenge and got A's and B's as a sophomore. I was humbled by my first semester at Loomis Chaffee, but went on to be a steady honor roll student. When I was accepted to Middlebury College, I knew that it was a success gained in large part by my year away in New Hampshire. In my first semester of college, I again was humbled, but I am well prepared to rise to the standards set before me. Our year away from it all let me come back to my old life with a new understanding of myself, and a new drive for success.

Spring
Reimagining of School and Family Life

It's hard to say how this whole idea evolved. When my husband's school offered him a sabbatical, we reeled from the options before us. We could study, go abroad or try new careers. We could show our young sons other regions of our country, historic sites, and country life. We could even extend our summer and stay in New Hampshire, where my family had a cozy, lakeside cabin. Jeff and I were homebodies, but when the time came to accept one of the best benefits offered by our profession, we wanted to make the most of it while still maintaining a comfortable family life and appropriate educational standards for our boys.

We seemed to have just recently achieved the lifestyle we always desired. Having moved into our first private home, after living in dormitories full of rambunctious students for all fourteen years of our marriage, we felt settled at last. I had finally returned to teaching full time, after raising preschoolers while attending graduate school in special education. Jeff had recently joined the administration at his school, adding college counseling to teaching history, dormitory parenting, and coaching football, baseball and hockey. Our sons, in fifth and eighth grade, enjoyed a vibrant cadre of friends and couldn't conceive of leaving them to be new kids in a new town. And what would

9

happen to their academic progress? The prospect daunted us all.

But in the words of my hero, Helen Keller, who first sparked my interest in teaching children with special educational needs, "Life is either a daring adventure or it is nothing." So, we embarked on our greatest adventure as a family and our greatest challenge as teachers. And I began to chronicle our year, for us and for anyone who ever dreamed of taking off for the mountains, of exploring the beauty of our beloved country or of teaching their children at home. In the peace of the mornings each day, before the family woke and we got to work, I began a routine of sitting with tea and writing about each step of the process we took in creating an educational life for our sons that might enrich their lives and prepare them to go back to school more academically skilled, more motivated and more determined to use their educations to pursue good in the world. That chronicle follows…

April 1996

Jeff and I have always dreamed of retiring to New Hampshire's Lakes Region, so it makes sense to spend his sabbatical there, to test the cool waters. We have friends who work at Holderness School, near Squam Lake, and they have repeatedly invited us to relocate near them. Always tempted, I long for my childhood home in the lakes region, for its tumbling mountains, glinting lakes, and soft, winding, pine needle paths. I long to share all these pleasures with my children and to give them something else, something that may no longer be up there. It is a calmer, more innocent way of life; one that I took for granted before moving to the bustling suburbs of Hartford. Still, I don't want to disrupt the boys' school lives. I like how settled they are in Windsor. They have good, kind, energetic friends and they work hard in school. Nor do I want to disrupt my just burgeoning teaching career just because Jeff can. But I trust that perhaps this decision will make itself, if we can just listen and follow.

Frustrated and deeply concerned, I don't know what's best for Tim anymore. He struggles in fifth grade, reading at a second-grade level, and insists, "No, mom, I'm not just saying it; I really *hate* school!" He has been lost in his class of twenty-four students where his teacher refers to his immature handwriting as "hieroglyphics," and he has alternately aced and failed math tests depending on whether a paraprofessional has been available to read the questions to him. On his last test, he estimated the weight of a cucumber perfectly, but the problem asked for the weight of a computer. Such letter reversals and transpositions plague his attempts at reading and spelling. We have tried everything to help him prepare for weekly spelling tests: from flashcards at each doorway to chocolate pudding finger-paints in the tub. Repeated drill and practice with letter sounds he simply cannot distinguish or recall always leads to frustration and too often to failure.

Yet, attending his special education classes, where support with phonemic awareness is available, in some ways he has dipped further. Once he came home with a paper on which his classroom teacher had written, "Good Job!" next to a smiley face. He had only written three words where a paragraph was required. He knew it was not a good job! He ran in the house, charged up the stairs, and threw himself on his bed shouting; "I'm stupid! I'm stupid! I'm stupid!" He spat the words out between sobs, and I still cannot shake the image.

Often he regresses in the resource room where standards seem lower, intellectual competition is avoided and bullies are allowed to monopolize the teacher's attention. Bright kids need competitive intellectual discourse. They need others to challenge them to raise the bar for themselves. But in mainstream classes where Tim revels in the challenge, teachers have no time to address his needs, and he faces daily humiliations. Special educator M. Joy Wright laments the diminished school lives of students like Tim in her article, *Gifted and Learning Disabled*, "Many teachers aren't quite sure how to help these children: They don't fit into the gifted program because of their disabilities, and they don't fit into the resource program because of their giftedness... Too many of today's twice-exceptional children don't survive the system, and their raw talent is lost" (p. 49).

The world needs Tim's talents. So creative, he can build anything. But his confidence is already sliding, and without confidence, how will he dare to contribute his many skills. Tim avoids school. Too many days begin with a struggle, with tummy-aches and with jokes about heating up the thermometer against a light bulb to feign a fever. I'll never forget the looks on workmen's faces one morning after Tim intentionally missed the bus and refused to put on shoes to go to school. I walked him barefoot through the snow to our car. I was shaking – he, screaming. But he never missed the bus again, and his morning tummy-aches eventually subsided. Still, I feel like such a failure. I'm a learning disabilities specialist and worthless to my own child. I want to provide the one-on-one reading instruction he needs, but school is so difficult for him already. How can I drill him some more when he gets home? Wrestling through homework challenges our relationship enough, especially when I push him to recheck his spelling. "I have to work twice as hard as anybody else in my class!" He is not mistaken. And still, he needs time to relax and play as much as, or more than, anyone.

A year in the mountains may be the answer. I would have to give up the work that I love and one half of our family's income, but what might we gain? We could try to teach Tim at home. There he could be free. Free to delve into learning his way: from nature and experience, like researching how to construct a lean-to or writing down his vivid dreams. Like John Rogers, chief of the Chippewa nation, Tim "could learn much more from the smiling, rippling waters and from the moss and flowers than from anything the teachers could tell [him] about such matters." Tim loves to write in resonant detail and his stories are mesmerizing, albeit illegible to most. He simply has no efficient method for getting his ideas on paper, and he can't always have his parents taking dictation. Homeschooling may be the answer. We can offer him the one-on-one instruction schools cannot. We have ordered a word prediction program for the computer, to help him record his thoughts independently while predicting the words that he intends to spell. With such technological assistance and direct reading instruction, we'd like to level the playing field for him in school. But I am concerned about teaching him myself; he plays me like Nintendo.

Our older son, Matt, has my number too, and he doesn't need an extra year of school. Academically, he is ready to attend the demanding college preparatory school where Jeff teaches. In fact, he needs the challenge. But he is only thirteen and unaccustomed to the intellectual demands he will face at Loomis Chaffee School.

He has wallowed in underachievement: quite the opposite of Tim. Anonymity has taken its toll. In a middle school with twelve hundred students from five neighborhood elementary schools, he has grown bored with his studies and confused about how to behave. His lunch money has been stolen, once by knife-point at his locker. He doesn't always care about his work, because he has no close relationships with his thin-spread teachers, suffering from annual budget cuts. At a recent meeting his math teacher said, "Matt is so thoughtful and such a whizz at algebra, he would be perfect if he would only get his homework in on time." He is my absent-minded professor, and I bit my tongue on the question, "why should he be perfect?" When he was younger, he hungrily sought intellectual stimulation. I remember him reading the Kmart and McDonalds' signs when he was only three and keeping his reading light on too late throughout elementary school. Now he has lost interest in books, and his writing seems stilted and immature compared to his storytelling, like someone has blocked the passage from his thoughts to his fingers on the keyboard. I wonder if he tries to downplay his innate intellect to fit in. He often completes assignments that he never hands in. Once, during the carpool home, he forgot I was driving and boasted to his friends about how little he studied for a quiz, insisting that it was stupid anyway. I hate that apathy has grabbed him so early in his schooling.

It's a battle to get Matt to express his good ideas on paper. He obediently completes his homework each night but seldom cares about his work. I do. I'd like to save his stories, but he often throws them out. I nag him to study and prod his teachers to keep after him. I tried to help him with his last paper, to get him to develop a thesis beyond his effortless relay of encyclopedic facts. "It's good enough!" He nearly tore it out of my hands. Apparently it was. He got an A.

Maybe a year away will help him rediscover his natural curiosity and drive to pursue more than good-enough self-expression. Maybe he will enjoy writing to friends and to himself. Maybe we can share books and literary discussions. Though he does not admit it freely to his friends, he still loves books. If nothing else, he will be free to read and play baseball. He wants to develop his solid skills to become a great catcher. He has dogged determination on the field, just like his dad. We would love to see him direct to his education a third of the devotion he directs to baseball.

As for me, my special education career is just taking off, so how can I leave my students now? I had a great moment with Whitney this week in my resource room for sixth graders. She completed a persuasive essay with "And that's all I have to say to you fucks." It didn't sound like Whitney, an extremely sweet and naive sixth grader. So after class, I asked her to read it to me. She was pleased. "And that's all I have to say to you folks," she concluded. When I explained to her that she had spelled a bad word, she turned pink-skinned and giggly. When she suddenly guessed which one, she turned a shade pinker. Then we spent some time together, hunched over colored markers, decoding folk and yolk. She was so intent on getting it right. There it was: the authentic learning moment. I wanted it to go on, but I was late for a meeting. Hustling away, wishing that we had more time to giggle over spelling conventions, I knew she would not forget that lesson any sooner than I would.

One of my middle school students announced that he wants to kill me. He said it last week in front of the secretaries when I sent him to the office. They were alarmed and alerted me after they reported the incident to the assistant principal, and she did nothing. They were shocked; I was livid. For three days I stewed over what to say to her. Even if I had been too strict with him, he needed help controlling his behavior and his classmates needed a safe and quiet place to learn. They all deserved clear and consistent standards. Too often this boy's teachers, afraid to confront him and to battle his will, had tolerated his rude outbursts and swearing. He was intimidating. Last month he threw a rock in another student's window at home, almost hitting a three-year-old cousin. Last year he burned an expletive in another neighbor's yard. Now he bragged that he had a gun. He was probably just talking, but given his history, I felt uneasy.

I finally spoke to the assistant principal. Narrowing her eyes, she asked, "Are you afraid?" I wanted to say yes, perhaps just to make her hold him accountable, but it wasn't true. More to the point, it wasn't the issue. Why do we let kids say anything as long as they don't act upon it? Words clothe our souls. She wouldn't let him wear a hat in school; why would she let him threaten a teacher's life? She didn't get it. She was afraid to respond if his behavior might have been caused by his disability. He had been suspended for too many days already. Legally, another suspension would deny him equal access to an education under the Individuals with Disabilities Act – an act I fought to enforce every day. Of course, she shouldn't withhold educational services, but threatening behavior can still be addressed. Failing to teach him appropriate behavior, she still denies him an appropriate education. Failing to support me, she surely denies my students a safe and productive classroom for days to come.

The next day he came into class triumphant, disruptive, and unwilling to work on his writing. It's too bad. He has haunting stories to tell, and the energy to tell them provocatively. After a year of encouraging him to write forcefully, to pour out his strange ideas, I felt utterly defeated. But not by him. Hence, it will be easier than I expected to resign and free myself to take a sabbatical with my family. Rather than look for a teaching position in New Hampshire, perhaps I can afford a respite and a chance to teach my kids at home. But how will we get by on one income?

June

At my fifteenth college reunion I enjoy hearing our vivacious president speak. Claire Gaudiani has brought Connecticut College to unprecedented national recognition as an exemplary college and now speaks powerfully about the art of teaching and learning. She stresses that nothing is more important than "faculty spending time with students, in a time when schools are calling on faculty to do so many other things." I know this to be true. I know that if we do homeschool the kids, the coming year will spoil me for teaching in a way. I will never again have such omnipresence in my students' lives. Gaudiani describes great examples for me to emulate. Recently, two teachers and twenty-one students traveled together to India with little preparation, so the "faculty modeled what it is to be an active, open, permeable learner of another culture." Closer to home, students and faculty made 36" by 36" plots in the campus arboretum to study the ecosystems within. My journal is filling as fast as the boxes I am packing in my classroom, I jot down these two new ideas for my year with the boys.

It is always great to see my college classmate Jennifer, who started a Montessori school in her home when her children were young. She offers a realistic perspective on what it is like to teach one's own kids. Excited for me, she offers words of encouragement, her revelations reminiscent of M. Scott Peck's words:

> The more children know that you value them, that you consider them extraordinary people, the more willing they will be to listen to you and afford you the same esteem. And the more appropriate your teaching, based on your knowledge of them, the more eager your children will be to learn from you. And the more they learn, the more extraordinary they will become.

I want to let my children know what extraordinary things they can do.

Another classmate, Mike, who, like me, dabbled with poetry in college, has become, like me, a teacher of writing and has a young teenager of his own. Talking on our old dormitory patio that overlooks the playing fields and distantly the Long Island Sound, he empathizes with my urge to teach my own children, to impart my love for the art of writing in particular, the art my oldest has found so elusive thus far in his schooling. Mike mentions his efforts to have a poetic biography of Michelangelo published and, recalling my son's interest in such artistic inventors as Leonardo DaVinci, I encourage Mike to send me a copy. What a boon if, through this non-traditional, nonfiction approach, I can interest Matthew in poetry, art, invention, and Italy. Later, reading the opening poem, which so wrenchingly describes Michelangelo's despair as he held his dead mother "like a newborn in his arms" with "pieces of his family lying broken by the bed," I feel inspired to write as well.

During an annual checkup, our family doctor, Renee, points out that a patient had encouraged her children to write and send their favorite postcards home from their trip across the country. Thereby they created a wonderful book of memories that was waiting for them when they returned home: I love this idea and will store it away for the cross country trip we want the boys to plan for our homeschooling winter term.

It's funny how life falls into place when we let it. Soon after I decide to give up my job, Marion – the dean of academic affairs at Holderness School – calls. She asks if I will work with some of her students with learning disabilities next year. That will bridge the financial gap, and still leave us free to travel some. Then a colleague calls a friend who offers to rent us her spacious summer home in Holderness overlooking Squam Lake. It isn't available until fall, but Marion and her husband have accepted a travel grant to Italy and need us to house sit for the summer. It is on a quiet, green and blossomed lane aptly called Garland Street. We have agreed to care for their cats, so with ours, we will have four! It should be cozy.

Summer is the best time to be in New Hampshire's Lakes Region: my time. I visit for the weekend, and something in the air, the friendliness of the people, the enveloping mountain views, makes me feel more comfortable in a completely strange community than I have for ten years in suburbia. As Matt said years ago, when we picked him up from Camp Belknap, nestled in the woods of Wolfeboro, "Mom, have you noticed how much calmer I am here?" I had noticed, and I notice that feeling in me now.

Already Jeff has begun coaching a summer baseball team for Matt in Plymouth, so we have headed even further north for their first doubleheader. Matt makes a good showing. He hits a long one, 300 feet, and best of all, it is caught! The level of play and coaching are going to be a good match for him. The coaches have already lined up players who would like to put Matt up for a few nights if necessary before we move up from Connecticut in July. During a lunch break between games, I comment on how nice the boys seem. "Yeah," Matt nods, his soft brown eyes opening wide. "Really nice!" He and Jeff have been warmly welcomed by the kind of folks I grew up with, the kind of folks who, like me, say "jesum crow!" or "wicked awesome" in every third sentence, especially in response to one of Matt's solid hits or to Jeff's consistently sharp pitching at batting practice. Comforted to know that some of the buoyant style of my childhood neighbors remains alive in New Hampshire's lake towns, I settle in to watch them play ball.

Encircled by mountains and eager knickered ballplayers, Jeff is in his element. On the baseball diamond my husband connects with the universe. There he tends his fields as his Amish ancestors did; there he imparts a sense of belonging to youth. It's nearly religious, his reverence for the game and for the field, God given. Pitching to his players, he looks so young: teasing the boys through batting practice, hoofing the musky earth under his cleats and grinning at the next batter, "You haven't seen my heat yet, have you?" He pauses to smell his vinegary leather glove, then launches one low and inside.

Perhaps I am a little envious. Jeff and I used to tease and play together like that, but parenthood and professionalism have taken most of our energies of late. It's no one's fault, no point of contention, just a reality of our busy, fifteenth year of marriage. Most of our recreational time is spent taking turns with our kids. I hope next year will give us the time and space to rediscover our common interests and passion for each other's company.

So, we will move to Plymouth this July and stay on the mountain as long as we can make it up to the steep hilltop in snow. We want to ski and homeschool the kids, then go on a country full of field trips to mountains and museums across America. The kids will help plan and budget these trips: good life skills. In January, we will enjoy a leisurely Christmas with our extended family in New Hampshire, then in Ohio. From there we will travel to Colorado to ski the Rockies and to see life out west. In March, we will explore the east coast down to Florida where Jeff has been hired by his friends, three brothers and ex-major league ball players, who own the Draper Baseball School. It's a dream, a sketched-out plan, a commencement.

On my birthday I am wistful. Just being at my family's lakefront house in Wolfeboro feels celebratory. It is exhilarating to struggle with Mum and my brother Dan to put the docks into the cold lake. I laugh, a little sister again, every time Dan hops out of the water squealing, "What was that?" It turns out to be a fifteen-inch-long catfish nipping at his toe, through the hole in his old Keds. With masks on, we discover it is guarding a golden, sandy nest of eggs. Like Anne Morrow Lindbergh in her famous day at the shore with her sister in *Gift of the Sea*, I revel in the simple silent companionship of my mother and brother as we lift huge, granite rocks into old, submerged, pine cradles that support the docks my children will run and dive from all summer long. Like the catfish, we are nesting, preparing for the rebirth of past summer joys.

But this summer won't be quite so rushed as others. We can linger at the lake well into fall, studying the nesting habits of so many creatures. Dan, assisting in the homeschooling effort, describes in great detail to the boys a snapping turtle he found squashed in the road and the eggs he feels sure will not survive, previously buried in the roadside sand. He helps Tim to scrounge out all the parts of a dismantled sailboat, and they start to design a raft Tim plans to build, innovating to stay above the cold water and nipping wildlife. As no one else can, Dan appreciates my effort to school the kids at home. Due to his learning disability, my parents had him repeat the ninth grade before he entered Phillips Exeter Academy. I do not think he was ever convinced that Exeter was a great choice for him. He struggled alongside the best and the brightest students in the world at a time when no one really understood how such an intelligent student like he could fail to read or spell. Plus, he was wiggly; asking him to go to school for an extra year was asking a lot. At least Tim's extra year will be a change from the frustrations of his present school life.

Tim learns best, as Dan always has, hammering found objects together or looking deep into a lake through a mask. While hoping his own brother won't shove him in on top of that eerie catfish, Tim observes its thorned fins and sharp looking whiskers protruding from each side of its long, dark frown. I hope that a year of learning through experiences like this will build Tim's confidence and revive his natural curiosity. In turn I hope he will return to school next year refreshed and ready to learn from the books that stump and alienate him now. They are two peas in a pod, my brother and my son. Like Albert Einstein, who had a hard time in school, their achievements clearly support Gardner's theory of multiple intelligences, a theory that gives us such high hopes for Tim, whose spatial and kinesthetic intelligences shine brightly. Indeed, Einstein showed that, as he taught, "imagination is more important than knowledge."

Before leaving for Italy, Marion throws a block party to introduce us to the neighbors. Her friend, Maryjo, an effervescent teacher at Plymouth State College, asks about our plans. When describing how our sabbatical had fallen together, I am at a loss to explain our good fortune. "It was Grace." I muse, surprised I have said it out loud. Marion flashes a knowing smile and nods. "Of course," she turns to Maryjo matter-of-factly and agrees, "it was Grace." How suddenly and accidentally we bond with good souls. I think what I came to give my sons still is here in the woods of New Hampshire.

B ack in Connecticut, the special services team at my middle
school throws a surprise bon voyage party for me. They seem so
giddy as they pull out their gifts, a planned collection that includes
an elegant scrapbook and matching journal. It is a daily planner and
a writer's journal full of inspiring quotations from Woolf, Twain,
Emerson and Steinem. I think I'll blow some up and frame them by
my computer for inspiration. Perhaps I shouldn't have told them that
I'm hoping to write a book about our experience; now the pressure's
on. Margaret Atwood's confession comforts me just as the forgiving
title of the book, *The Good Enough Parent,* did when Matt was very
young. "If I waited for perfection...I would never write a word."

Our celebration is sprinkled with talk of how one of my students,
a boy bussed from the inner city whose gradual grin could make my
day, was beaten by his mother in the school office when she came to
pick him up for a disciplinary offense. The Department for Child and
Family Services was called, but no one expresses optimism that any
good will come of it. I am horrified to hear that his mother actually
trains foster parents and has four foster/adopted children in addition
to her two natural sons. When the chant begins, "speech, speech!" I
choke up, partly with tears of appreciation for my colleagues' support
through times like these, but also with odd relief. I feel relief finally
knowing why this conundrum of a kid, so slow to smile but eager to
please, has soft, hurt eyes that sometimes glaze over in a fog of apathy.

Our school psychologist, who has also researched homeschooling,
expresses my own concerns so eloquently, it frightens me. "Oh,
I decided I could never teach my own children. They've got my
number. I could never get them to do the work!" Well meaning,

she hits an exposed nerve. Tim refuses to read with me at night, as if having witnessed my panicked reaction. I fight exhaustion at the end of the day. "Oh God, don't test me now," I pray silently. Firmly and repeatedly I tell him to turn off the light. "If you're not reading, neither am I. That's the deal." Finally, he reads one page. I watch his eyes. He is reading, but his eyes bounce all over the page, tracking the words as best he can while searching for other clues in the title, a picture, previous sentences and sentences to follow. Brilliantly, he scans the page for clues when his faulty reading gives him inadequate information – brilliantly, but inefficiently.

His approach to reading is so cumbersome. His mind is so sharp. The combination is cruelly frustrating. How will I help him streamline this approach, accept the imperfection of his literacy? His disability is compounded by his perfectionism. He wants to know more than the author presents, and he assumes, from years of failure, that he just fails to grasp it all. He doesn't realize that no reader comprehends everything on a first read, but that the author, through repetition of themes and images, always reinforces what is essential.

Students make such surprising gains in their reading scores when allowed to focus what stands out for them; what is naturally memorable. It seems to give them confidence, being able to grasp whatever strikes them in a reading, rather than looking for answers to questions they think a teacher might ask. It allows their reading and their responses to be so much more personal. Perhaps this is why I could not get myself to read *Pride and Prejudice* when it was assigned in high school and again in college. I remember looking for the story line that my teacher followed and trying to compare Austen's writing style to Emily Brontë's. It was not until I was an adult that I devoured the book twice in a week. First to find out whether Mr. Darcy was a decent man, and again, to relive his romance with Eliza Bennett, with whom I identified. I hope that choosing their own approaches to great literature will allow my kids to identify with a few rich characters like I did with Miss Elizabeth Bennett's warmth, humor, and integrity. Thinking of Austin, I am again prodded to try my hand at the writing I hope to do on our sabbatical. I peek at Tim, sleeping softly with none of the day's frustration on his smooth, sweet face. I cry on paper:

Dyslexia
Tramping up the stairs,
Stomp,
      Whack,
            Stomp,
                  Whack,
I lug my backpack behind me,
                        Dreading
its contents spilling out onto the floor
with heavy tears,
and I kick at the books
that taunt me.
I dive onto my bed shouting,
"I'm stupid,
      I'm stupid,
            I'm stupid!"

Knowing that this she will hear.

But I barely hear her footsteps beyond

the pillow,

my wails and

inadequacy.

Her hand touches my back

cool,

     soft,

          yet trembling,

and I heave anguish at her,

striking her hard with the truth.

"I can't read, and I never will!"

She waits out my tears,

then, finally,

slides next to me,

sharing my pillow and pain.

I brush off her hair

and her voice

     nearly breaking,

          Reads:

"It was a terrible, horrible, no good,

very bad day..."

I close my tired eyes

and see every word

against their lids.

July

After a long, hard day of packing, cleaning and "when in doubt, throwing it out" – one of my friend Sarah's mantras – we are finally living in Plymouth. I wake at 5:30 in the morning, the sweet smell of last night's pork chops and strawberry pudding lingering in the air. I slip out from under soft, cotton sheets and pat four waiting cats and a dog, pleased with how they are getting along. It is cool and damp and my roller blades make a high whizzing sound as they roll over wet pavement smooth enough for me to enjoy several spins around the block. The neighborhood is full of green flowered yards and nineteenth century bungalows. Later – after sipping Irish Breakfast tea on the porch while our yearling golden retriever, Brittany, runs the yard and Jeff's coffee brews – I stroll down to Duell's Market for apples, muffins, and the paper. It is pronounced "mahket" here, a familiar sound. Jim, the owner, sure to be a friend, tells me he opens officially at eight-thirty, but if the lights are on after seven, the door is open. It's hometown.

A neighbor who attended Marion's party, recommends me to work with a friend's son who has a learning disability and will be entering seventh grade next fall. What a windfall. This will help keep my skills fresh and help pay for the boy's summer camp. Later, another friend of Marion's, Sally, skips up our path to invite us to her Holderness School faculty "Wet Wednesdays" each week. Thus, I am professionally and socially set for the summer.

Later, at my brother's home in nearby Concord, Matt and Tim play relentlessly with their small cousins as if we have deprived them of the blocks and Lincoln logs they abandoned and handed down years ago. I love finally living so close to our extended family. Madeline, at five, repeatedly demands that Matt sit by her, teasing out his winning grin. He becomes distracted, though, by two-week-old Becky. Prematurely paternal at thirteen, he monopolizes her with a sheepish smile and tender hands. He marvels at how much help she needs to support her head before any of us remember to tell him. Then he scrunches up his nose whispering, "Mom, she's as big as my head!" He already proved he was a natural with small children last year, when he was sledding out of control and a two-year-old toddled across his path. Rather than crashing, he simply swooped the child up, cooed at her, and they slid down the hill together, giggling. Relieved, the child's mother turned to me and said, "He has quite a way with kids, doesn't he?" He does.

One morning Tim lets himself be cajoled into signing up for the Plymouth public library's reading challenge. This may sound pretty mundane, but not to a parent of a 10-year-old with a learning disability. For this child, it represents a major advance. He chooses to read six books at the first to second grade level, a modest goal, but a face-saving, guaranteed success. Fine. What blows Jeff and me away is that, for over an hour after we get home, he reads two of the books and enthusiastically shares their plots with us. Lesson learned, interest level is more important than reading level and low reading level books increase reading confidence and fluency. A great learning morning for both home teachers and kid.

Meanwhile, Matt's been reading local guides, and at his suggestion we spend the afternoon as a family exploring the Mad River at Thornton Gore, a pine tree enclosed river rushing down the mountain. So much wilder than our soft, sultry rivers in the flatlands, it sends chills up our backs as we step into its sparkle and hear its roar. Water splashes down a tumble of rocks, creating pools and rivulets and a fresh mist in the air, like the stinging spray of shaken ginger ale. A hot day, we brave the glistening waters, and melt like hot fudge over ice cream. Slowly, painfully, we sit down into the rushing water. Then, like an icy jacuzzi, it pounds our backs and soothes our shoulders, pink from the sun.

AUGUST

Summer in New Hampshire has become an impressionist blur of activity and relaxation. Jeff has been wrapped up with coaching Matt's Babe Ruth baseball team. Too soon for me, Jeff and Matt have flown to Florida for four weeks of baseball camp, after which Matt will return for only one day on his way to two weeks of YMCA camp. We have never been apart for that long, but aside from missing Matt's newly low-register laugh and Jeff's companionship, I find I quite enjoy my simple, new life. I feel doubly guilty for this, because I complained intermittently about their going. But Tim and I keep occupied with our new next-door neighbors. Maryjo and her son, Spence, just Tim's age, love trips to the half-pipe in-line skating rink at Waterville Valley. The boys display such impressive feats there that we have posters made of the snapshots I take of them doing heli's and ankle grabs. How proudly they announce, "That's me!" when friends visit their rooms.

Dropping Matt and Tim off at our beloved Camp Belknap three weeks later, seems easy at first even though Jeff remains in Florida, and I have to juggle packing, labeling clothes and picking Matt up at the airport all by myself. Matt is happy to be back and says a quick, loving goodbye at his beloved camp of four years. My more wary Tim, a new camper, is immediately whisked off by a gang of cabinmates, leaving me to wander down to the waterfront to see the assistant camp director, Ryan. Our sons have known him as "Uncle Ryan" since Jeff and I worked with him at Belknap the year before and the year after Matt was born. Back then, Ryan coined the term "Matt-therapy" when we would all take turns cuddling and playing with nine-month-old Matt whenever we needed a boost or a break from weighty camp matters. It is so good to see him again and to know he'll be near the boys for the next two weeks.

Hugging Ryan goodbye and turning to head up to the cabin to take my leave of Tim, I am stopped at the door, met by the tear-stained face and shaking body of the little boy I must catch and release effectively to Ryan's steadfast charge. Gently pulling Tim out of my arms, wiping his face with my fingers and kissing his still cherubic cheek, I turn and stride away, as if it's no big deal. Still, my stoic smile holds only until I am out of sight. Driving down the dusty camp road, I can barely navigate through my own tears and shaking body. I tell myself that Ryan has Tim playing tetherball with his buddies by now, yet in my arms I still feel his small soul, frantic and frightened, and I cannot let him go.

Left pervasively anxious for the first day and entirely alone for the ensuing week – a first for me since college – I send off all the letters and care packages I can without risk of making my boys homesick, then decide to go camping by myself, another first. I have always longed to go but never dared go alone. Jeff and Matt prefer hotels with ESPN and a pool to tents and bird calling. I think Tim would enjoy camping though, and the others might enjoy the novelty as well as his antics. Perhaps if I give it a try alone, explore what's involved, we can go together on one of our field trips this year.

As I settle in at a campsite near a beach in Rhode Island, proudly surveying my roughly erected tent (success at last) and beautiful fire (always my forte), I wait for water to boil in a tin pan and ponder yet another kind of learning experience that my boys' sixteen other years of schooling may not offer. I begin to see the glimmer of a vast opportunity here. Perhaps I shouldn't be so gung-ho to recreate my classroom and its curriculum for my sons this year. Though I brought a full carload of textbooks, trade books, worksheets, and educational games – and there certainly is a lot of good stuff there – looking around me, feeling so expanded by the safe embrace of the woods, the tooting call of the birds, and the sooty smell of the fire, I feel there is something to be learned just being here in the quiet. What is it? I shrug to myself and hope that in the course of the next year we will all find out. I breathe.

I slowly sip tea in sweet seclusion and stroll a soft, breezy, boundless beach. Reading Anne Tyler's *Ladder of Years*, I feel like the heroine when she walks away from her family on a similar sounding beach and starts a new life. This life feels new and solitary too. Only I am not plagued by the protagonist's guilt. I have not deserted my family. They left me, for the time being, and yet, I don't seem to mind right now. Getting past a few days of yearning, it feels so light and free to wake up with fewer burdens. I still ache to hold my boys again, but I can wait a little longer and then hold them all the closer. Maya Angelo concurs. "If we step away for a time, we are not, as many may think and some will accuse, being irresponsible, but rather we are preparing ourselves to more ably perform our duties and discharge our obligations." We are also teaching our children resilience, so critical to their success. I know this, but my heart still yearns for my guys.

Days later, when I head to the airport to meet Jeff, I don't know how I feel about his return. I am still peeved at him for taking Matt and himself away for so long, seeming to put baseball before family. What does this teach our kids? This year is supposed to be about putting our family first. Maybe it still is. I don't know. Pinching pennies, settling Tim in at Plymouth, and doing all we can to support Matt's dream of becoming a great baseball player have become parental tasks best accomplished apart for a time. But what does such independence in a marriage do to our union and model for our kids? When I asked Jeff whether he worried about our separation, he shrugged, "Why should I? We're married." Stung, I still knew it wasn't a brush off, but an expression of his deep level of faith and assurance that we have each other. He sees no point in creating false expressions of the obvious. But I need more. His complacency is frustratingly masculine.

Jeff's flight arrives late, so I order a glass of wine while waiting. It is huge, and I am unaccustomed. I feel light-headed and spirited, like in church when I haven't eaten before taking communion. My rushing mind softens and by the time the plane arrives, I care only about seeing him again. Only a few weeks since the horrifying Flight 800 crash, suddenly and intensely I need him back. I push to the front of a crowd of people barred from the gate for new and unsettling security reasons. Then he serenely saunters through the gate like a man in a used car lot, blithely looking for a model just like his first car. So familiar, that serenity I loathe becomes the serenity I love again. Perennially dressed in his favorite khakis and baseball coach's jacket, he sees me and quickens his step. I respond, sinking into his arms in relief. Surprisingly unabashed, rather than characteristically patting and stoically pushing me upright, he touches my hair and breathes – centering on me as I center on him.

Fall
Homeschooling on the Mountaintop
SEPTEMBER

After such a busy and beautiful summer, it is good to be together, to take one another for granted again and to begin to create new routines. School started two days ago down the road for the town of Plymouth and simultaneously for us in our new home on the mountain.

Carefully selecting a routine for the homeschool day is our first hurdle. With a working routine for the boys to accept and anticipate, a thousand battles for control can be forestalled. When the boys awake, they turn on the news. With no access to cable TV or internet, just news and PBS, the options are limited, but we hope to make that an educational advantage, it certainly helps our budget. By eight o'clock a.m. they each quietly read mountain biking magazines and a guide from which they begin to cooperatively plan a ten-mile excursion up and down one of the foothills of the White Mountains. By nine they come downstairs for Maypo, then settle in at the dining room table to complete a folder full of academic assignments I have laid out and listed in their assignment books under the topics of reading, research, math, and French (for Matt) or spelling (for Tim). They also each have "dailies" to complete. Tim's includes process spelling, a close paragraph, silent reading, journal writing and multiplication facts. Matt's includes silent reading, journal writing and vocabulary development. Jeff and I run an instructional tag-team relay, one working with the boys when the other is out or each taking responsibility for one child or one subject at a time. Though we share common goals and a common workload, we seldom share individual lessons. Though fun, that would seem inefficient with two such different students, and we'd lose the precious one on one instruction we came here to utilize.

Already disrupting my plan, the boys have replaced my research selections with researching the geography of the trail they want to bike. To do so, they read from a book written at an adult reading level and apply the information they receive directly in the afternoon. Then they dig into all their other assignments, voraciously completing them by noon so they can go on their trail ride. On the way to the trail, I discuss adverbs with Matthew and sneakily discuss nouns, verbs, and adjectives with him for Tim's edification. The bike ride that initially threatened to occlude all my academic plans for the boys provides the incentive for the morning lessons and the greatest learning experience of the day. Not only do the boys get a great workout, but they also get lost and learn that, in the future, they must take their reference book along to reread directions and to seek clarification. How many times have I tried to get my history students to do just that? And when were they ever as motivated as my two boys, lost on an unfamiliar trail? Such self-directed learning is just what we came for.

Our second day is more homebound. Jeff oversees the morning lessons while I attend a meeting at Holderness School. Matt previews an algebra II textbook I brought home for him and selects algebra and French software from a catalog. I'll have to order a speaking and word predicting writing program for Tim as well. Matt researches skis, carefully comparing the affordable types recommended for his level and weight. He needs a new pair this year. How teenagers grow! I'm sure when my aunt shook her head saying that I could never make my children do schoolwork at home, she feared that the curriculum would dissolve in this way. It has indeed dissolved… dissolved to a curriculum that has my thirteen-year-old passionately reading from three separate primary reference sources, locating information therein, and applying that information to his previous knowledge of himself as a skier, his estimated and anticipated weight, height and budget. Now that he has the incentive to develop such critical thinking skills, he can easily apply them to any scientific or social study set before him in high school next year.

If the weather holds out, tomorrow, at Tim's request, will be Lake Day. After their "dailies," we will go to Squam Lake to study the perimeter, area, and volume of geometrically formed sand castles, estimate the number of grains of sand on the beach and use an algebraic equation (slope=rise/run) to determine the angle at which the beach drops off. Matt will have to teach Tim, and me, that one! We'll have to take the microscope and the pond life guide with us so that we can study any organisms we find in that ecosystem, as well. Now that's my kind of classroom! I am as psyched as the kids are to get out of the house and explore.

A chilly day, we postpone Lake Day and head to the Polar Caves for a family field trip. We feed deer and geese, and explore many caves created by a glacial avalanche during the ice age. Our guide provides an informative and interesting hike through the rock formations. We shiver and crawl quickly through the coolest cave, used as a source of ice through July for centuries. What a phenomenal place! The boys write in their journals about what it might have felt like to be a Native American boy hiding with his mother in one of the caves while the men were off defending their home from the Mohawks, and I wrack my brain and travel brochures for more opportunities like this. I would love to come up with a comparable field trip each week. Novelty is such a good teacher!

After entertaining company for dinner into the night, we get off to a slow start the next day. Even when we finally complete the dailies, we all seem to be simply going through the motions. Matt skips chapter one in his Algebra book but then has more difficulty than he expects with the chapter two pretest, leaving him defeated and reluctant to complete the first unit in that chapter. He needs a break, to get away from the source of his frustration and come back at it later, when he feels fresher. I try to redirect him academically, coaxing him to write in his journal about George Orwell's *Animal Farm*. I want him to stretch, to write on an abstract level, to make the intriguing connections he makes when we talk, but he just scribbles that it was just like *1984* and barely elaborates. I push, he pushes back. When he picks up *To Kill a Mockingbird*, I acquiesce and encourage him to read that, with the understanding that within the week he will have to complete a fully elaborated project related to that book. He retreats to his room to read, guaranteed success, promised peace. At least he makes good literary selections; I just hope solid literary reflections will follow.

Meanwhile, Tim receives a thoughtfully and painstakingly written letter from a sixth-grade student in Marta's class. My mother's best friend, she is an open and inquisitive special education teacher in Rye, New Hampshire and my long-time mentor. While our own parents maintain a wary outlook about how Jeff and I are going to make homeschooling work effectively for our kids, Marta characteristically cheers, and I think, feels a little envious of the opportunity we have seized. So, in that spirit, she has shared materials with me and encouraged one of her students to write to Tim. The kids have a lot in common, both academically and in their choice of sports and interests, so they could become lasting pen pals and great supporters of one another's reading and writing progress.

Thus, thanks to Marta and her student, I devise a great lesson for Tim around reading and responding to the letter. But Tim's onto us. He sends himself to his room for an hour, refusing to have a pen pal. I sit exasperated and steaming. I worry about the boy who won't hear back and my dear friend who so graciously reached out, but most of all I worry about Tim, about his fear of having an audience for his writing and his resistance to making the effort to learn to read and write effectively. I sit deflated and edgy, ready to make matters worse with both boys, when Jeff returns home from double sessions of preseason football practices at Holderness School. Despite his own exhaustion, he gets Tim going on a math assignment while I take a long deferred shower, then cradle a misty cup of tea on the porch, looking out at Squam Lake and, far off, the White Mountains.

Patches of bright red maples, the lake's view away, remind me of why we are here and restore my resolve. I breathe in the soft, sweet mist rising off my cup and off the simmering, musty forest. Matt, having had time to recover himself and joining me to drink in the view of Rattlesnake Mountain and Chocorua, leans against my shoulder gently and formulates a new tack. He suggests that we go to the library and research rock climbing. This has become a favorite new interest that he shares with Tim, especially since I just returned from hiking along Maryland's Appalachian Trail and climbing Annapolis Rocks with my best friend, Cath. The boys find it inconceivable that I scaled the fifty-foot cliffs. So do I, but I revel in setting an adventurous example for my boys and jump at the chance to share what I have learned about finding hand holds in rock crevices and providing a safe bolé. Am I just indulging my new passion? Am I allowing Matt to dodge academics? Am I setting the right tone for the year? Is this enough like school? Does it need to be?

So, after the boys complete Jeff's hilarious, ice-breaking push up and sit up challenge match, we all head for the library. Once there, we find more books on kayaking and mountain biking than rock climbing, and Matt chooses a Stephen King novel, perhaps as a break from our more classic selections. Why not? I resist the voice in the back of my head warning that I am getting too lax, too soon. Interest level is vastly more predictive of reading success than reading level. Tim begins passionately planning an instruction booklet on kayaking that he will write and illustrate. He is saving up to buy a kayak, such freedom for a ten-year-old. Matt considers researching and designing a mountain bike and writing a promotional flyer for it. So, they are motivated, if not entirely structured. No more just going through the motions! At least for now.

Several weeks in, setting goals and keeping to a consistent schedule are the issues with which we struggle most. The kids are accustomed to being motivated by teachers, peers, rules, and an absurdly fragmented, but tightly structured, public school schedule. Last year, Matt's school had nine distinct class periods a day separated by bone-crushing five-minute passing periods in crowded halls and a morsel-choking twenty-four-minute lunch break. Now we begin the day slowly, but intelligently, watching and discussing *The Today Show* together, reading silently from books, magazines or the newspaper, and completing daily assignments that vary in content but not in structure. This routine helps us to get through half of the learning that I want my children to accomplish each day from the get-go. But our more abstract, beyond the rote, learning objectives are so much harder to achieve. Indeed, they are harder to formulate. The goals I want to set for my children are important but won't lead to their best effort or be fueled by the intrinsic motivation of the goals that they set for themselves. But will they challenge themselves enough? Or will they overreach and become discouraged?

Fueling my desire to entrust their educational goals to my boys, Dr. Spencer Johnson and Constance Johnson's book *The One-Minute Teacher* gives me a way. Interestingly, the author of *The One Minute Manager*, a renowned doctor and writer, has teamed up with his sister, a public and private school teacher and lecturer on education, to create this book for teachers. Their parents, it is clear from the dedication, were both educators like mine. The authors express concern about "the reality of overworked teachers and underachieving students" (p. 110). This has long concerned me as a public school teacher and even now as a teacher of my own children. Students need to be the most active participants in their educations. Jeff and I are finding that as we work with our own boys, we need to worry less about curriculum and more about creating learning moments whenever they come up. Johnson's thesis, nestled in the idea that "rather than give a hungry man a fish, it is far better to teach him to fish for himself, then he will have food for a lifetime," inspires and directs me. I want to teach my kids to fish for knowledge for a lifetime. According to the Johnsons, there are three steps that I must teach myself, and then my boys, to use regularly. These include one-minute goal setting, one-minute praising and one-minute recovery when we get off track. The book is brief and compellingly written like a fable. After I practice using the system myself, I might read it to the boys as our cozy, evening, read-aloud book.

Tag-teaming works well for Jeff and me. By the time my energy peters out after news, reading, and dailies, Jeff takes over and instructs

Matt in the algebraic determination of the slope of a line (slope = rise/run) and then teaches Tim to add and divide to find an average. Tim, who struggles so with reading, asks if he can see the horror film *IT* if he reads a chapter of Matt's Stephen King book by the same title. Still debating whether this is a good decision, I determine that it is worth the nightmares he'll surely suffer when, leaning warmly against my side, he fights his way through words like "insurmountable" (which is for him) and "impassable" (which he figures out!). I could not in a hundred days have come up with a more challenging and motivating reading and phonetic decoding lesson for him. Struggling with just those two words, he has learned the meanings of the prefixes in- and im-, the suffix –able, and the root words "mount" and "pass." He has heard the effect of a double consonant on a vowel and the sound made by the devilish digraph "ou," and he has practiced accenting the correct syllable in multisyllabic words. Whew!

After lunch we set off to the Science Center of New Hampshire fortuitously located at the base of our hill. We can use our town library pass to explore it free of charge anytime. Tim, our animal expert, is psyched; Matt isn't so sure. It's so hard to balance the interests of an energetic child and a restrained adolescent. But we spend three hours there, fully involved in the exhibits and hiking the trails. Tim and Matt seem equally impressed, eyes wide, feet flying from one exhibit to the next. We see black bears, deer, bobcats, falcons, etc. We learn how careful the keepers are to maintain a healthy ecosystem for the animals and how proud they are that their captive animals were all rescued, being unable to survive in the wild due to a variety of handicaps. Tim grabs my hand and pulls me along to see the blind snowy owl and the wounded turkey vulture as he figures out why they have been brought to the Science Center, why they couldn't fend for themselves anymore. We walk a good three miles through the more naturally inhabited woods around the center, enjoying an integrated science, language arts, math, and gym lesson along the way. "This was really fun!" Matt admits as we leave. Jeff and I share our awareness that he originally agreed to go only to avoid more stagnant forms of research or French review.

G randparents worry, as well they should. Taking the boys out of school for a year sure has given our parents plenty to worry about. They worry that the kids will be lonely, that they will miss and need daily contact with their peers. And I worry that they're right. That our experiment will fail. And at what cost? Fortunately, they have now seen the boys playing on their football and soccer teams in Plymouth this fall, and they have checked out the Saturday morning classes in pottery and archery that Tim and Matt may take. They have also seen what good friends these brothers have become for each other. Admittedly, this has been by necessity. Other peers are not as readily available. For all their school years, this might be stifling, but for one year it feels like a great investment. After all, this is the only relationship likely to last their whole lives, and we can influence the strength of that bond now.

Our parents also worry that the kids will manipulate us and fritter the year away, forgetting all they have learned in school. They worry because, like us, they do not know where or how they would begin to school their own children. And yet they did it. When I was a child, I remember my dad reading Homer's *Odyssey* as a bedtime story. He made this story, otherwise far from my grasp, so real as he referred to "Susy of Troy" to my delighted squeals of "Read it right, Daddy!" Even now as I write, I still hear my Dad's professorial voice insisting that I write down my thoughts, "Just say it, Suz!" Throughout my childhood my mom clearly and matter-of-factly answered every question I ever asked or helped me find the answer. Even when I was a teen and there were certain questions my friends could not ask their moms, we all knew we could ask mine; we knew where to go for the facts. Teaching was so natural to my parents; they couldn't appreciate what a gift it was. But they seem to appreciate what a gift it is to the boys.

OCTOBER

Our commitment to spending more time with family continues as Jeff's parents visit for the weekend and mine come for Tim's soccer game and Matt's birthday celebration. It's the peak of "Leaf Peeper Season," and they love the view from the porch atop our mountain as we sip tea and munch cookies that I suddenly have time to bake regularly. They all enjoy the boy's dinner-table display of their new vocabulary and spelling skills. They pour over the boys' journals, enjoying Tim's description of his favorite character, the Centipede, in James and the Giant Peach and Matt's elaborate discussion of his evening at the Red Sox game Tuesday night. His idol, Cal Ripken, a generous ball signer, passed him in the crowd, but then shouted, "Where are the kids?" to which Tim shouted, "I'm a kid!" and got his ball signed. Matt's cruel fate, always to be the sweet, big brother

Risk! Risk anything! Care no more for the opinions of others, for those voices. Do the hardest thing on earth for you. Act for yourself. Face the truth.

- Katherine Mansfield

to an assertive cutie-pie. Cake and presents naturally include new ski boots for Matt's fast-growing feet. Before leaving for home, my dad asks to take a copy of our fridge-posted homeschooling schedule to show to my aunt, a retired first grade teacher herself, who has voiced the most concern about our plans, while simultaneously offering all of her classroom materials. How classic that our parents, who tried so hard to dissuade us from this adventure at its first conception, now stand stalwart to defend our right to do it and to brag about how well it is going, most of the time. As ever, I don't want to let him down.

The following day, our new teenager, Matt, plays football in front of all of his grandparents and half our town. I always love watching him play. He is strong and smart. Inevitably, being Matt's mom also brings me reflected glory in the stands, a gift as a newcomer in a small town. He takes a handoff as fullback and plows over several players and under the goal posts. There, he forgets his father's favorite adage; "when you get in the end zone, don't act like you've never been there before." In unrestrained, youthful glee, which fills my heart and wells my tears, he pitches the pigskin into a fence at the back of the end zone. Penalty: fifteen yards. Lesson: humility.

No one should attempt homeschooling without becoming a member of a science museum. Before the Red Sox game we never had time for before, we visit Boston's Museum of Science and, by becoming members, pay the equivalent of two visits for unlimited visits to it and to about a hundred other museums. What a deal! Since we hope to travel this year, we plan to milk this for all it's worth! Our town's library passes have opened even more doors to us.

At the museum the boys enjoy a fascinating visit. We are all mesmerized by the Omni Theater presentation of how the film industry creates special effects. Matt wonders if he would enjoy being a researcher for filmmakers. Tim finds himself drawn to a career in pyrotechnics. Heaven help us! It is intriguing to see how the specialists create explosions such as the demolition of the White House in the movie *Independence Day*. We think Tim is more likely to pursue acting since he performed for one of the computer video shows related to Newton's laws of gravity. It provided a wonderfully interactive way to get kids involved in physics. I certainly have never visited a science museum without learning something new about science and effective teaching.

As the boys take more responsibility for their own learning, we find it possible to relax into the routine of homeschooling. They still complete their dailies in the morning, and Jeff, normally a history teacher, has created a beautifully structured math curriculum for each of them to follow. Tim passes his test on geometry, but remains impatient when he does not get everything right. Perfectionism is a heavy burden that I hope he will set down. It paralyzes him

When the soul is present, nature is alive.
Thomas Moore

sometimes. Other times it is a gift, making him a whirling dervish of active learning and a great innovator.

After math time, Tim and Matt devour the chapter on camping in Beard's *American Boy's Handybook*. Then, they spend the afternoon hiking half a mile into the woods and setting up a campsite. They clear a soft, mossy area and put up our little tent. When they create a ring of stones for a campfire, I am impressed by how conscientiously they have dug out a sandy pit and the area around it, saving the excess dirt to put out the fire at night. I have to admit, they are being responsible. They even have dug out a small latrine. Clearly, they have done their homework. Warm inside and happy for the time to ourselves, Jeff and I chuckle watching the weather forecast: rain is coming overnight.

Sure enough, in spite of rain and nighttime temperatures that dropped below thirty degrees, when I hike out to wake them in the morning, I find the boys, all bed-headed and just stirring from their damp pillows in their tent. Their food is still carefully lodged in the branches of a tree nearby in an effort to keep bears away. This is not a frivolous matter. We have seen a bear just a few miles away, and I heard a moose calling early one morning. In fact, upon waking, noticeably happy to see me, Matt bravely relates that he heard several animals during the night, and one made a repetitive clapping noise that may have been the rubbing of antlers against a tree. We have seen one white-tailed doe with her fawn, so this makes a good guess.

Thus, our structured lessons have given way to lessons only children immersed in nature can create.

The mist beyond our deck finally rises after the rain, exposing Squam Lake and all its islands in the valley below and the barest outline of Mount Chocorua in the distant northeast. Sipping from my favorite, loon mug, I feel as though I belong in a tea commercial. Could I ever take living up here for granted? The sunrise to the right of the foliaged mountain threads through the brightening sky with pinks and blues and yellows above the white sliver of mist that rises off the lake. This is a writer's paradise. Margaret Mead and Rollo May summered on this very hill to write. Mead's words support our decision to spend our sabbatical winter exploring America: "Be grounded in your own culture. Know who you are, and know what your culture is all about." They say that when she visited other cultures, the anthropologist always kept her free hand open when she was writing. She did this intentionally, to express her openness and friendship toward the people she met. I hope we have met people here with the same open hand; they certainly have met us that way. As I write about our neighbors, about our small town culture and about my favorite anthropologist, I hope Mead's inspiration still stirs the brisk air.

If so, Tim has caught it. He reads, yes, on a Saturday morning, he reads! And by choice, he researches in *Boys Life Magazine* how to make a fireplace outdoors and asks me to inspect his before he tries it out. Three months in and the boy who from first through fifth grade wasn't responding to interventions provided at school is now reading, voluntarily. Perhaps this free fall approach to learning is working after all. His fireplace is symmetrical and solid, like a miniature, cement-free version of the tall, rustic rock fireplace and chimney in my grandparents' garden. My father built it during the summer after he returned from active duty as a lieutenant in World War II. I have often wondered if that project wasn't therapeutic for Dad as he readjusted to civilian life following his efforts in the Pacific. How odd a juxtaposition: his thoughts then, and the thoughts of his ten-year-old grandson today, standing on the other side of innocence. I hope they talk about it.

Matt will want to listen in. He is starting a project on the emotional toll of the Vietnam War. It is not surprising that he has chosen this topic. He read Tim O'Brien's *The Things They Carried* and several of Michael Sharra's books over the past few years. They moved him. Now he has so many questions to answer – essential research questions, and most critically, it is the search that he will learn from, the process. In the spring, he will lead us through the Vietnam Memorial in Washington, on our way to the circuit through Civil War battlefields that he has asked to visit. Our library has a copy of the PBS Civil War series that we will view first, start to finish. War is not my favorite course of study, but my commitment is to the boys' interests, not mine, and Jeff has great expertise in this period of American life.

Tim continues to pursue an interest in lizards. While scrounging up rocks for his fireplace project, he found two red striped newts. We have a good field guide from which he identified these newest members of our menagerie. We already have two cats, a dog and a tropical lizard. Is this an inquisitive scientist in the making? But do we have the resources and the expertise to support his interests?

On a jaunt to the library for information on lizards and the Vietnam War, the boys embark on a veritable safari with their librarian at the Holderness Free Library. She shows them her down home collection and queries, "What is your best resource in a library?" My mind races thinking: the card catalog? The reader's guide? The computer? "Me," she simply states. "Your librarian is your best resource. Don't be afraid to use it." I smile at yet another local stranger so willing to share her gifts with my boys. In the course of our visit, Tim triumphantly finds ten resources on lizards and Matt finds eight on Vietnam. The number is significant, because at the penny candy store afterward they each get to spend a dime for each resource they have found. Our librarian is so impressed by how directed they were in their searches; I am reluctant to tell her they were being bribed. But heck, bribery makes it more fun, and Matt always picks up an extra Tootsie Roll for me!

These competitive boys have had a ball with timed readings. Who would have thought it? I have found that most of my students read much more effectively and without distraction when they increase their reading speed and learn to read in phrases. Tim reads at about 110 words per minute, Matt at about 200. The high school average being well over 200, they could stand to improve a bit and, in turn, that will shorten almost every assignment they ever have to complete. By timing them as they read for one- or five-minute intervals, I find them reading more intently and increasing their speed to as much as 170 and 270 words per minute, respectively. That's a 65 - 75% increase! This they accomplish with very little loss in comprehension. If the new speed becomes habit, their comprehension level will not only recover because they won't need to concentrate on speed reading, but may improve because they will have less time for distracting thoughts and will focus on phrases and meaning more than individual words. No wonder variations of this technique have been used so widely with groups from executives to students with learning disabilities.

> *Obstacles are those frightful things you see when you take your eyes off your goal.*
>
> - Henry Ford

After a rainy weekend, we face another rainy day and a trial. The boys have been bugging each other and, frankly, me, all day. For a break from our usual routine, and to help us suffer the cold, we wrap up in our Amish quilts and huddle by the woodstove to watch a documentary on the Vietnam War. Their homemade caramel popcorn and cocoa help as the boys have learned to accept home movies, four television channels, and other conservation techniques to get by on our reduced income this year: another valuable lesson.

The documentary is comprehensive and stirring though the boys struggle to determine how to respond in their journals. Student scores for writing in our old home district were perennially abysmal, and we can see the results. Our kids just don't know how to talk on paper. Mind, these boys can talk! If we only free up their written voices this year, it will be invaluable. Afterward, Tim goes out to play and Matt remains to watch *Pride and Prejudice* in the Arts & Entertainment video series with me. I love this story! Jane Austen presents romantic and yet comically cynical and capricious descriptions of English society. While enjoying it in spite of his assumption that it would be just an old-fashioned "chick flick," Matt also has occasion to hear many words one seldom hears in present day conversation. He asks about the meanings of terms like "keenly" and "consolation." Tim even joins us after a while and sparks an excellent discourse on life in the eighteen hundreds when he blurts out, "What wimps! Why would they be tired after riding in a carriage for fifty miles?" Matt condescends, "You try it!" How exuberantly our callow historians throw themselves into the life and times of those they study.

A visit to paddle around Squam Lake is cold but still beautiful. Afterward we wrap up in sweats and sit outside. The view from our deck is spectacular with color that has washed into a soft watercolor painting with the rain. We have had three days of downpours. The boys remain responsive to homeschooling, but it is hard. We all have to be so dedicated and diligent. Tim is on his third book by Roald Dahl; what a great writer to catch his wild imagination and sweetness. He readily chats with me about the characters, takes short turns with the readings, and writes journal responses, letting his own imagination run as wild as Dahl's – so cool. Matt has returned to reading Harper's *To Kill A Mockingbird*, enriching his interest in law and civil rights and writing an excellent essay that explores how the women in Scout's life affect her development. Jeff teaches so well. He has mastered the art of task analysis, separating the assignment into five separate paragraph lessons that he then asks Matt to draw together into one solid, cohesive, but initially not intimidating five-paragraph essay. I have much to learn from this gentle teacher I married. Meanwhile, Cath, my best friend from birth and Appalachian Trail hiking partner, teaches Matt French by mail and occasional phone calls. Utterly unable to help, we are concerned that he will forget all that he has learned of the language in the last two years. This distance learning approach challenges both of them, but Cath has a great teaching style and a generous desire to take part in our experience. The bonus is that we now have an excuse to keep in touch regularly.

For weeks now the boys have been helping to plan our trip out west after Christmas. It has been a shared task and a terrific curriculum for them, as they try to get the most out of our vacation time and our restricted budget. We have been hampered by our inability to afford an Internet set up from a server that is a toll call away. Friends say it would be a huge boon to our homeschooling plan, but I am skeptical and a bit overwhelmed by this new technology and the monthly fees. Through more traditional channels – stopping by the travel agents', making a few calls – Matt has discovered a unique opportunity offered by American Airlines and Amtrak. Flying out, then taking the train back, we have our choice of three stopping places on our return. So, first we will fly to Salt Lake City, Utah to do a bit of research, then ski at one of the great canyons. Then, we think we'll take the train to Glenwood Springs, then Denver, Colorado for the Hot Springs and more slopes. From there we may go to a Native American reservation and artist colony in Taos, where Matt wants to ski some more, or we will visit the many ski areas in Summit County, Colorado. I am going to be sore!

Here in Holderness, just twenty minutes from the White Mountains, we will ski almost daily this winter. To feed our pastime, the boys have been studying sports nutrition, and pumping up our breakfast proteins. Matt cooks! Bless his home health and economics teacher for teaching him to prepare eggs. I am not an egg lover, so it is a relief to delegate this task to Matt, while Jeff and I organize all our skis, poles, helmets, goggles, gloves, gaiters, and snacks into the car. Tim makes toast and sets the table. We have invested in season passes and look forward to sharing this passion as a family. A friend once told me, "skiing was the glue that held our family together through the adolescent years." It may work as well for us. These days we are all obsessed with running to the deck to check the tops of the mountains for the first snowy peaks.

I now am working with several students with learning problems who attend Holderness and loving it! It's great to serve kids who struggle in school and to make my own hours. Through their studies, I have enjoyed re-experiencing Hawthorne's *The Scarlet Letter*, O'Brien's *The Things They Carried*, and Conrad's *Heart of Darkness*. They're great books that I hope to share with my boys, too! This change, from public school teaching with nine class periods a day and a caseload of over forty students with complex needs, to working one on one with motivated students attending a private school where teachers have time to confer with me over lunch, is a dream come true. Alone with each student for a full class period, I can teach so many strategies that will enhance their independence and self-awareness as learners. I struggle with the economic inequities and offer my services pro bono to students on financial aid, but still wonder. After this year, will I go back to the public schools in hopes of narrowing the educational equity gap or continue as I have just begun, free to meet the needs of my students effectively each day.

I have lately had the honor of being asked to give a chapel talk at the school. I am basing it on the story of *The Velveteen Rabbit* who had his fur "loved off" and became real in the eyes of the boy who loved him. Enjoying the same collaboration we relish offering the boys this year, Jeff helps me write the talk. Then, just before I have to leave, I can't find my notes anywhere. I search the house in a tizzy, looking under papers strewn throughout the study, on the coffee table, all across the dining room table, our homeschool headquarters. Jeff rescues me again, finding that my notes had fallen behind a cabinet. He brings our sons to their first Episcopal school chapel service to listen with the school community. They enter solemnly, and I begin:

Becoming Real at Holderness

A year ago, I first saw Holderness. My son had arranged for an interview, because the school had a great football program, a strong academic tradition and skiing. Plus, it looked great in the catalog where students smiled out at us from every picture framed by technicolor trees or pristine snow.

But now that we're here the leaves have fallen and there's not much snow. That catalog impression has worn off. And yet to quote my own prep school English teacher who retired up here, "I find Holderness friendly as an old shoe." And like you, I am beginning to find ways to fit in. Holderness has become real.

I learned about becoming real on my wedding day when our minister read to us from *The Velveteen Rabbit*. Fifteen years later I am really glad he did, though I am starting to resemble the Skin Horse. "... Generally, by the time you are Real, most of your hair has been loved off, and your eyes drop out and you get loose in the joints and very shabby. But these things don't matter at all, because once you are Real you can't be ugly, except to people who don't understand."

How fortunate we are to be in a place that is real enough to allow you the time and space to discover your gifts and to give them freely. The world won't always be like that. But when it is you will know you are loved. Of course, love is a two-way street, and catalog impressions do become tattered. So, when the weather is gloomy or your teacher seems "so unfair!" and the Holderness experience just isn't quite what you expected, smile. You may just be falling in love.

While it is possible that our family has overused this particular literary selection, it is as well received as ever. As well as it was when the Reverend George Booth, who baptized me as a child, chose it for the sermon when he married Jeff and me back in 1981. As well as it was the following year, when Jeff used it for a moving, kid-friendly chapel talk at our beloved Camp Belknap. There he shocked me by stating to three hundred boys what he always had been rather shy about telling me – that he loved me and always would in spite of how

I might change over the years. How happy that made me then, given that I was enormously pregnant with Matthew at the time and felt quite "loose in the joints and very shabby," not to mention rather flabby. I like the moral of the story more every year.

The students and faculty greet me and my family warmly after chapel, and the boys seemed proud to sit with me at dinner as people come up to thank me. I had been scared about giving the talk, but am glad now that the boys got to see how rewarding it can be to take a risk and invest oneself in a new place to become a part of it. I hope it is a lesson that will stick. They have grown up in the same town since they were toddlers, and we're so grateful to have been able to give them that stability. However, this year in a new town teaches them, teaches us, that we can be happy anywhere if we reach out and create community. Our new school, our new teams, and our new church have been terrific sources of common ground, fellowship, and fun, allowing us, very quickly to feel at home in the mountains and quite tempted to stay forever. Even the boys, who don't have the natural daily connection with other kids that school would offer, already have a bevy of friends from soccer, football, and church school who end up at our house for lasagna dinners (mom has time to cook now) and raucous overnights.

We're back to our dailies in the morning, and then a family excursion for the day takes us to one of those condominium sales presentations offering a free trip to Cape Cod in exchange for our attendance. What a learning opportunity! The boys marvel at the resort and try out the game room. They watch the video presentation with us and share in our discussion of the pros and cons of timeshare vacationing. As easily led as the ideal customer, they ogle the brochure of all the resorts we could visit on the timeshare's exchange program, neglecting to consider the cost in light of maintenance fees, exchange fees, and loan interest rates. Then, suddenly guarded, they become as uneasy as we do when the salesman continues pushing after we politely say we are not interested at this time. They share our dismay when he complains that we only came to take advantage of the free trip we were offered. Well yes, that was what led us to fill out the card at a country fair weeks before. Bait and switch advertising threatens to turn ugly. Now, not only do we not want to invest $15,000 at this time, but also, we do not want to do business with this operation, ever. The kids get it. Later, over lunch they read the fine print on the free vacation offer that brought us to the presentation in the first place and conclude that most people would have an extremely difficult time using it due to all the restrictions imposed. Indeed, they learn that there are no free rides.

A similar lesson presents itself. Though leery, we allow Matt to write in for an opportunity to "make money at home stuffing envelopes" that he read in an ad in the newspaper. He never receives a response. Soon afterward he counts himself lucky when he reads more about such scams and finds that they work like chain letters and other "somebody has to lose for you to win" propositions. A good life lesson: cheaply learned.

Life in the foothills of the White Mountain National Forest offers spectacular vistas and visits. The sun rises in a wash of pink and gold glistening on the frost-speckled woods surrounding us this morning. The leaves have created a thick, ruddy carpet on the ground. Through bare branches, I view all three lakes below us now, both Squams and White Oak Pond. The half sun silhouettes a crimson Red Hill that lives up to its name and a purple Mount Chocorua. Meanwhile, to the north Rattlesnake Mountain shines silver in its light. Clumpy clouds create the image of lesser hills across its surface, and suddenly the bald shine of the White Cliffs catches my attention. It awakens the haunting memory of a story our friends shared last night as we sat sipping wine on the porch while soup simmered, and all our boys explored the trails around our mountaintop haven.

I shiver now, recalling the horrible accident a local family suffered on those cliffs a few years ago. Hiking with five other families one chilly morning, their walking was slowed by younger children while all their pre-teens ran ahead, thrashing beyond their parents' sight. Suddenly, the soft silence of the forest was shattered by screams. Five fathers charged down between the large rock formations of the cliff. One of the boys was missing. He had slipped off the edge of the icy cliffs. When they finally reached him, forty feet below, they found him sitting in a heap where he exclaimed that his feet were broken and that his back was killing him. They would later discover that both legs and feet were broken in multiple places and a vertebra in his back was pulverized.

In high school, he remained athletic. However, since his injuries limited his full ability to play soccer, he chose to ski instead, perhaps because the boots provided extra support for his ankles. Knowing him now, I find this sweet, smart boy has a good soul, and is remarkably positive and gentle with others. He writes his college essay about a poster his father gave him in the hospital. It pictures a frog being swallowed by a pelican. It tenaciously grasps the pelican's long neck to prevent it from swallowing, even though the frog's head is fully in the pelican's mouth. The caption below says: "Never give up!" I don't know if I could deal with such a catastrophe with his strength and still impart such essential humor and optimism to my child. I sneak in to give Matthew a good morning hug as if he were a child again, and he lets me.

Sharing the stories of other parents makes us stronger parents, stronger teachers. It shows, again, that it does take a village to raise a child. That sense of community, and time, has allowed us to appreciate our children's gifts more than usual this year. Our boys exude joyous buoyancy. They and their buddy Spence have set up the tent in the living room. It's hunting season, and we do not want them camping in the woods. So, last night, three, and tonight, six, kids sleep soundly in the tent after gooey Tootsie Roll sundaes, a house shaking game of 'hide and go seek'; and a tent shaking game of Twister. What could be regarded as quite annoying, certainly unsettling, is simply joyous. Jeff and I go to bed wondering how lucky we are to have safe, happy kids who find "camping in" cool and entertaining.

Tim wears us all thin some days. During spelling he discovers that he does not distinguish the short "o" from the short "u" sounds. It is a frustrating discovery, because when he finds that he is wrong to guess "o," he guesses "u" on the next word and is wrong again. The next thing I know his whiteboard marker is careening through the air, and he is buried under his favorite afghan on the couch refusing to uncover his head shouting, "You don't know how to teach!" I fear the truth in what he says, and consider the implied threat that he would be better off at the town school with teachers he would have to be more tolerant and respectful toward. Piaget teaches us that frustration is necessary for new learning. Well, here it is. I wonder whether we have made a monumental mistake. Does he need to be working with a reading specialist? How much can I really teach him of a skill that I struggled to learn myself in school? Yet, his difficulty provides a monumental discovery too. Finally we know precisely what vowel sounds he must learn to distinguish from now on. If I persevere, will he?

We know that such work is paying off. Using parts of the Woodcock Johnson Tests of Achievement, I assess the boys' progress to date. Though I have no previous testing to which to compare Matthew's scores, he scores above the twelfth-grade level on every test except the reading comprehension section, which is still well above his eighth grade level. He confidently attempts every selection, and makes good choices. A good test taker and a competitor, he reviews his scores and decides to concentrate on improving his reading comprehension.

Tim also demonstrates far more confidence than in the past, though he still needs some prodding to stick with a problem and "to give it a guess." His guesses ultimately hit the target. He learns what Matt has always known about testing: give it a shot. His fifth-grade math scores show improvements in calculating, though he still chooses repeated addition to multiplication and that slows him down. His decoding skills have improved but remain below grade level and indicate a need for further remediation, no surprise. His reading comprehension score has skyrocketed since May though: from a 3.6 to a 5.9 grade point level. Much of that, I believe, has resulted from his willingness to take a guess on the test. He has also benefited from his self-directed research, family reading hours, and the timed readings he has been so newly willing to complete, allowing him to read freely and energetically and to focus on the message of a short story, not each word in isolation.

Still hooked on Roald Dahl's books, Tim reads without undue hair-pulling now. The latest, *Fantastic Mr. Fox*, engages his imagination and his ability to see things from many perspectives. He eagerly completes a diorama of the main characters battling over the farm as a final project, accentuating his right-brained creativity. He is a builder. Matt, meanwhile, reads John Knowles' *A Separate Peace*, and at its conclusion plans to visit its setting, Phillips Exeter Academy, for an admissions interview. As the dean's daughter, I was raised there, schooled there, and my parents still live in town, so his interest delights me as much as it alarms me to think of him going away to school at such a young age. As a dormitory head at two different schools, I have always thought that my adolescents would stay home under the care and watchful eye of the two adults who know them best.

Matt's admissions interview with my old English professor must have gone well. Though initially leery and transparently convinced that homeschooling would not prepare a student well enough for PEA, after meeting with Matt, Tom emerges from his office enthusiastic about our homeschooling enterprise. I catch him unobtrusively testing Matt with questions about the books he's read. Satisfied, he recommends several other books, which Matt promises to read in the weeks that follow. It's convenient to have a grandma who works at the school's bookstore.

Later in the day, my father discusses *A Separate Peace* with Matt. He has taught at Exeter since returning home from his naval service during World War II, the era of the book's setting, and he brings that time to life for all of us. Together, we hike out to the tree that Phineas and Gene jumped from in the story. To find it, Tim has estimated its size based on the fact that fifty years have passed since Phineas supposedly fell from it. Matt and his Gramps delve into a debate about Gene's "jostling" the branch. Did he intend to make Phineas fall? Could the branch on that tree be jostled and cause a boy to fall on the bank with a force that would break his leg? Dad is still a penetrating teacher and scholar, and Matt is a chip off his crusty, old block. I love to listen to them talk.

Out there along the river, under the trees, I recall my own prep school days when Dad once came to my room seeming nervous and serious. He told me that he had been asked to take over as Dean of the Academy, and he wanted my permission. My permission. I was stunned. I didn't realize then what an impact it would have on me. I was just so honored that he would ask me. "Of course. Congratulations, Dad! You'll be great." He was great, and I showered in reflected glory. I also became a much more serious student and leader, perhaps in an effort to be a credit to him, to his station. Though less academically capable than the majority of my classmates, I struggled my way to graduate with honors. Night after night I stayed up writing draft after draft, sometimes until the birds sang outside my window, just to write papers that paled in comparison with the work that I saw my classmates type out at will in one natural, flowing draft. Being the dean's daughter also added enormous weight and significance to my every social movement. When I walked out of the Academy building holding hands with a new, nervous boyfriend, Dad's voice suddenly bellowed behind us, "Hey, hey! What's going on?" My hand was abruptly dropped even as dear Mr. Smucker, a younger faculty member, grabbed Dad's arm and led him away chuckling, "Nothing that hasn't been going on for years, Don." I am glad he was amused; I was mortified. Now I watch my son and my father, heads upright, looking out over the water as they discuss the historic war between nations and the literary battle between boys; how easy and unfettered their relationship is. I wonder if Matt should go to Phillips Exeter rather than to Loomis Chaffee where he will not have to contend with the pressure of having his parents and all their friends on campus, noting his every move.

Yet, I recall more often being proud of my connection to the hierarchy of the Academy. In particular, I remember racing Dad home from his office one day, down the marble stairs, through the Ionic columns, beneath the austere buildings of the academic quadrangle, and past the astounded expressions of my peers and his. I laughed and jeered at him over my shoulder yelling, "Stodgy old administrators can't run!" He, a runner and a competitor, caught me at the door, and we burst breathlessly into the house, side by side, rapt in each other and in the glee of the moment. Dad's presence and Mum's were a constant source of strength and guidance during those demanding years. I want Jeff's gracious guidance and my steadfast support to be readily available to Matt throughout his high school years as well. But he has seen the Academy, its overwhelming beauty and magnificence, and he wants to be chosen to attend. "Mom, every dollar that could be spent on education has been spent here." So fortunate that this is an extension of home for him, that his grandparents still live here to provide support, discipline, and warmth, that he has the ability to make the most of this bastion of intellectual growth. I want to give him the chance to be educated as he chooses. Time will tell.

Who knew that Halloween would teach my kids to eat their vegetables? Chip, our local farmer, has a vegetable stand I have been raiding all summer. I have dusted off the old Moosewood cookbook and started making butternut squash and apple soup and homemade tomato sauce. All I have served alongside Suz' Bread, my version of a healthy anadama. Was that really named for a woman named Ann who made "a damned good bread?"

But I digress, again. So, we stop at Chip's stand – always fun for the kids. They pick out tomatoes and zucchini, munch on fresh, leggy beans, and sweet carrots, and buffet Chip with questions about farming and plants. He's an impressive botanist! But this time, he gives them a sneak peek of the Halloween barn that he and many of Matt's football buddies have been building. He invites them to come. I hesitate, and Matt points his finger into the air and spins it. "Whoop, whoop, whoop." Yup, I am a helicopter parent.

Both boys can barely stand the suspense as they wait for Halloween night, a chance to connect with some of the kids they've met through our work and at baseball and football games. They inventively design and redesign costumes, with rather little to work with. In the end, we spend most of our trick or treat time on the Holderness campus, going door to door with our new colleagues and their children. It's such a safe and engaging way to go trick-or-treating. With no roads and known families, it's a lot like at home. We run from dorm to dorm, faculty apartment to faculty apartment, and see colleagues with children in their own homes, often for the first time, but not the last.

Winter
Learning Across America

NOVEMBER

On the road for Thanksgiving, the first in a series of trips we want to take to visit loved ones and new destinations this year, our extended family and friends lovingly provide their own authentic lessons for our kids. We start by staying over with my good friend, Sarah, back home in Windsor, Connecticut. There we spend one crackling fire, soft rug, dog on our laps, knitting, laughing, listening evening as we take turns reading aloud *The Most Dangerous Game* in front of the fire. An uncompromisingly student-centered teacher, Sarah likes the idea of such a relaxed and homey classroom for our kids and understands the challenges and rewards we have faced. Sharing the enchantment of General Zertof's treacherous island with Sarah's kids, especially their best friend, John, I know the boys will not soon forget that night. Nor will I.

Now on the outskirts of Youngstown, Ohio, the Rosses treat us to dinner at a Mennonite farm in honor of Jeff's mother's Amish heritage. The farmhouse stands stark and gray against square, flat acres of green winter rye and brown tilled earth that stretch beyond our sight in every direction. Children in white shirts and black knickers play in the yard and enthusiastically announce our arrival. At a long, bountiful table, we gorge on roast pork, applesauce, fresh corn and beans, shoofly pie, and our new favorite, strawberry tapioca. Each of us discreetly leaving money under our plates, we slip away at sunset, watching the sky turn from gold, to pink, to indigo blue as the striking silhouette of a dark horse and buggy rambles along a straight road parallel to the bright horizon, plain and simple. In the evening, my mother-in-law stitches a quilt as I knit a sweater for my niece, and I understand the sweet serenity of living as her foremothers lived.

Next, we take off for South Bend, Indiana where our friend, Rick, shares his coach's tickets with us so that we can see the Fighting Irish of Notre Dame play Rutgers. At Denny's before the game, the boys have me paint a blue and gold ND on their cheeks and ask again about the men in kilts who dance during the halftime show. Indeed, the level of play and the pageantry thrills us all, as does Notre Dame's 62 to 0 victory, but the greatest thrill and lesson comes from coach Lou Holtz's address to the student body after the game. He speaks of the greatness of the school and how fortunate he feels to have been a part of it and to have graduated three children from there. He describes how he loves the institution as much as he loves the game. His last home game as the Irish's head football coach becomes a historic moment in football. Later, we retire to the College Football Hall of Fame to put that moment into perspective. What a great museum full of interactive experiences. Tim challenges the football skills test battery and Matt tries out sportscasting, recording his reactions on a video of Doug Flutie's famous Hail Mary pass. His fascination and facility with sports information as well as his good guy looks could lead him into broadcasting; what fun to watch him try it out here. The thought and inspiration that goes into each museum we visit impresses me.

On the way back to Jeff's parents' home in Ohio, we enjoy visiting the Toledo Zoo. The boys' zoological interest supplements our historical interest in that the zoo was built as one of the work projects of the New Deal that revived cities like Toledo under Franklin Delano Roosevelt's presidency. Later in the week, the lesson becomes an extended unit when Jeff's father, a one-time steelworker, gives us all a tour through the labor museum celebrating the steel mills that were once the heart of Youngstown, beating life and livelihood into the region. A consummate educator for the IBM corporation for decades, he provides his grandchildren with a vivid, personal account of the rise and fall of the steel mills after the depression, of the labor unions as they impacted his experience, and of the strong bond between football and the steel mill communities. Tim's eyes light up wide, when his Papa tells how when he was cut to the bone by a steel spike, he was cared for on site, in the mill's infirmary and not allowed to go home until closing time so that the injury would not be counted against the mill's safety record. Thus, the children obtain a firsthand account of the hardships of working in the corporate steel mills just as protective labor unions began to gain strength and power.

At night at Grandma's and Papa's, we watch the movie *Rudy*, a story of a young man like Papa, who gives up working in the steel mills in Gary, Indiana to pursue his dream to attend Notre Dame. Successful in spite of many setbacks, some caused by his learning disability, Rudy demonstrates the rewards of hard work. A powerful example of resilience and grit for Tim, struggling with a similar disability, and for Matt, a youth football player endeavoring to attend a big-time football college someday. It is going to be a family favorite.

Our greatest cause for thanksgiving comes in a tiny package. We meet and hug and spoil our three-year-old niece, Grace Tundee, newly adopted by Jeff's sister, Lauren, and her husband, Dean. Distantly kin to many of Youngstown's Eastern European steel mill workers, Grace is a Hungarian immigrant from a derelict Romanian orphanage. Meeting her, experiencing all her energy and joy, and seeing the pictures from Lauren and Dean's trip to Budapest to adopt her, offers a great cultural lesson that the boys embrace. I hold her in the sweater I started knitting the day Lauren and Dean flew to Hungary. Given a piece of bread, she always wants two, one for each hand, and she drinks a cup of milk down at once, a habit, we assume, developed from years of deprivation. She and Matt make fast friends. Toddlers always trust him, and well they should. He has a gentle and generous manner with them. Tim entertains her with airplane rides on his knee and whole-body shivers that she mimics, squealing, "Shaky, shaky!" Soon she thinks that's his name. But I most enjoy watching Jeff hold her in his arms. He becomes so utterly absorbed in her nature, and she, so comfortably settled in his lap, looking up into his eyes with deep chocolate brown irises, eager to know him and the world better. They listen to each other's foreign sounds as if each word carries the secret to happiness. Even Tim's energetic antics don't lure her away from the comfort of my sweet husband's presence.

Finally, on our way back to New England, we stop near Wappingers Falls, New York to explore Jeff's childhood home. At nearby Hyde Park we tour F.D.R.'s home, completing our lesson on his nation-defining presidency and the initiative of the New Deal, on which our present and future national security depends. We enjoy, in particular, the extensive collection and interactive programs in the library and museum on the grounds of his home, nestled in the soft purple and orange leafy landscape of the Hudson River Valley in autumn. Tim's plan of the moment is to own a restaurant someday, so the nearby Culinary Arts Institute of America provides us an opportunity to show Tim a college he might like should he ultimately choose to pursue his interest in cooking, soccer, and beautiful locations. But it is Matt who seems quite taken with the place. All in all, we have enjoyed a remarkable vacation to every corner of Jeff's childhood that mixed an integrated homeschooling lesson with the pleasure of visiting his extended family. I wonder how we will get the kids back into a homeschooling routine back home with Christmas so close. I wonder whether we need to. We are all learning so much from shared experiences, from setting shared goals and from researching ways to achieve them. We feel no rush to push the kids forward in school next year. We just want their time to be well spent, for them to grow in character, in strength, in compassion, and in intelligence.

Inspiration, hunger: these are the qualities that drive good schools. The best we educational planners can do is to create the most likely conditions for them to flourish, and then get out of their way.

- Ted Sizer

December

Back to the grind, albeit with less intensity than in the fall, partly because we have settled into a routine that the boys accept and expect, partly because they have taken over so much of the curriculum planning by taking charge of their research selections, task analysis, and timelines. Their ownership makes teaching more like coaching, a practice we strongly have advocated ever since Jeff began reading Ted Sizer's books in graduate school. We embrace his love of essential questions and student-centered learning.

We have just returned to our mountaintop home in Holderness after a day of skiing. We all have midweek season passes at Loon Mountain Ski Area affordably provided by our town's recreation department, and we are making the most of them! Some of our homeschooling will have to spill over into the weekends to make time for this singular opportunity. Motivated to work so that he might ski again next week, Tim makes cookies, cutting his recipe down by one half, which requires him to use many of the functions of dividing and making mixed fractions that he has been studying in his math text. The mail brings Matt his graded French papers from Cath who has carefully corrected them and pinpointed his areas of strength and weakness. She has filled a real void for us with this correspondence course. However, he still needs more exposure to the language. Fortunately, the "French in Action" program that Loomis Chaffee uses is being aired daily on PBS starting in ten days. We are indebted to PBS for this program as well as *Bill Nye the Science Guy*, *National Geographic* and *Krats' Kreatures*. PBS provides us a fine educational resource that the kids especially enjoy after an exhausting day on the slopes. They shower, rest, and watch while I stir soup, my new forté, and cut bread that I now bake twice a week: ah, the advantages of leisure. I have time to be the mother I could only dream of being back in my dial Domino Pizza days.

Nature, health, and physical education are the core curriculum this term, especially as we begin to hunker down for winter. The mountain bikes are put away, and the lake is ice cold, soon to be frozen. The boys are at an age where their bodies need movement, discipline and strength. And the natural world we've found continues to invite us to explore and to challenge ourselves. There's no healthier lifelong practice for us to instill in our children. So we ski.

As much as he loves our ski outings, Matt is determined to play basketball and the gracious Holderness Elementary School coach has invited him to join the team. This town has such a generous attitude toward homeschooling, and thanks to its well supported football program, Matt's athleticism has been noticed. Now he is even more determined to have a new, pricy pair of basketball shoes. Jeff says no before heading out to coach football this afternoon, but Matt's insistent whining wears on me, so I take the opportunity to put him to work writing a persuasive essay about why we should buy him the gaudy shoes. I warn him that a good persuasive essay includes a definitive argument with support, as well as a clear and respectful recognition and refutation of opposing opinions. My reluctant writer closes himself in the computer room and doesn't emerge for hours, when he presents me with a full four paragraphs, including the history of basketball as a sport created to keep athletes in shape between football and baseball seasons. That argument alone should convince his dad. And it does.

What have we done? Suddenly this idyllic summer vacation home becomes utterly inaccessible for my little car. A hard, early winter snowstorm hits over the weekend, and we have a rough time of it. Returning from working with my students Friday night, I need to pick up Matt for practice. But driving through our first real soft, sparkling snowfall that coats the trees with silver glitter, I narrowly survive two treacherous attempts to drive my car up the steepest part of our road. The tires spin and the car slips back and sideways toward massive tree trunks and a deep, threatening gully. So I give up, frustrated and frightened that we won't be able to remain in our mountain home. I retreat downhill to our country store, order tea, call Jeff, and nervously knit Matt's sweater, while Ed, the proprietor and all-around good guy, stokes the woodstove and opens its doors to warm me. I stew. Matt needs to get to basketball practice, and we can't get a new car. No way. A half-hour later, driving our heavy minivan with front wheel drive, Jeff drives Matt down from our house at the top of its steep and icy incline. Matt half walks, half slides down to me, waiting on the flatter, salted roadway below. He makes it to practice.

It turns out I was lucky I gave up. On our return, Matt and I come across a crash site. A car apparently plummeted down our steep road, clearly skidded over the opposite embankment and plowed into a tree ten feet below. It stands nearly upright on its front bumper, like a torpedo that has met its mark without exploding. It turns out that a young neighbor had braved driving down the hill, hit ice, and careened a terrifying fifty-yard-long slalom straight downhill, across the abutting street and into the woods. Thankfully, after catching her breath and checking for injuries, she climbed out unharmed; but wouldn't you know, her car was nearly new. There, right there, but for the grace of God, went I.

We drive past our road to our welcoming neighbors, Ilana and Bart, who encourage us to park our car in their driveway for the night. From there, the walk home with Matt through sparkling snow has that eerie, serene beauty of the calm before a storm. Yes, this particular storm is over, but it's only the first of a lengthy winter to come. We talk about practice, the kids he loves to play with, the cheerleaders who call him Rusty and how he misses going to school, being a part of that raucous world. This is good news. I tell him to remember this when he's older and hates his job. Work is a wonderful place to share common goals with others and to be appreciated for the part you can play. I thoroughly enjoy this time alone with my young man – just us in a new, hushed, whitened world. Impressively resilient, he does not complain about the cold, two-mile hike uphill, though practice already gave him a full workout. We simply share the wonder.

The next morning Tim has tryouts with the Loon Mountain freestyle ski team. Walking the two miles back down to our neighbors' home for our car at seven o'clock in the morning enchants even a sleepy boy. Suddenly Tim stops at the bend of our steep, half-mile long driveway where no signs of civilization exist. He whispers, "Mom, it looks like Christmas!" He's got a point. Except for our golden retriever's footprints and those of a rabbit and another, slightly larger animal, the ground, bushes, pine trees, and bare branches all stand sprinkled with a glistening layer of white powder. In the pinkness of dawn, it strikes me as a view through the rose-colored, starlight lens of a fine photographer. I love it. With a wink to my boy, I suddenly shuffle-run and slide down the hill on my boot-soles alongside Tim, laughing like schoolmates. Which, I guess we are, learning together how to live in a new world.

Upon our return from a tiring and busy Saturday skiing at the mountain and struggling with whether we can afford the time and money for Tim to join the team, we cannot drive up the hill, even in our front-wheel-drive minivan. A second storm hit during the day, dumping more ice and snow, so we must impose on our neighbors' driveway again and trudge home in the powder-flecked darkness. Typical of this neighborhood we now understand, our next-door neighbor has been called and soon picks us up in her truck and drives us the rest of the way home, saving us an exhausting two-mile walk and offering to drive us down to our cars again in the morning. "We've learned to help each other out, living up here through the winter." Dot shrugs. I finally crawl into my warm, down-comforted bed, feeling worn, stressed, and yet, blessed.

Morning brings a long round of calls. I stare wistfully at our beautiful view, at miles and miles of uninterrupted, shimmering, snow-covered trees, then icy lakes below, and then vanilla-frosted mountains beyond. I will miss this place. Now, can our realtor find us a new rental stat? Will our landlords allow us to cancel our lease? Will the electrical company transfer our service? Will the man we just paid to plow the long, uphill driveway all winter, plow for us in downtown Plymouth instead? Will we be able to move everything before another storm hits? I look around at our beautiful school room. Matt's books piled high and papers laid out. Tim's whiteboard, flashcards, and reference area. The room is a collage of their creations. How will we ever recreate our school?

Faced with a whirlwind plan, we pack up the house and move all our belongings into the back room of a rustic, eighteenth century home that is musty but mercifully on the main drag with no hill and only a tiny driveway to plow. We then zoom off to Exeter for a full week of Christmas with my parents followed by a week celebrating the new year at Jeff's parents' home in Ohio. From there we will embark on our cross-country trip. So many details to consider, on top of creating a traditional Christmas though away from home. What home? I reel.

With time to linger with relatives and truly no place else to go, we expand and enjoy the holiest of holidays, Christmas. Mum erases all the stress of the last week with her warmth and ease. The boys line up on the stairs with us, youngest first per tradition, bellowing to Gramps to hurry up. Jeff teases an antsy Tim, "Why?

Are the stockings getting cold?" Finally, they tear down the stairs and into the red tissue that cushions each gift crammed into white argyle stockings decorated with red, green, and brown Santas, candy canes, wreaths, and Rudolphs that Mum knitted during each of my pregnancies and, originally, during each of her own. While she puts the water on to boil for tea, I snitch one of her lemon-iced gingerbread men for breakfast, my favorite food. The kids work too fast and charge to the tree in the living room, which is suddenly, miraculously, lit up and loaded with presents below. They tear through gifts from Jeff's parents and from us, then struggle to eat and wait until eleven o'clock, when Aunt Connie and my brothers arrive, to finally begin the opening of the rest of the presents. Even then the cousins struggle to wait, New England style, for each family member to slowly open each gift and express their pleasure, one at a time. It is a tortuous process that we always hope teaches them to delay gratification and to focus on others at this time of year.

The red and white turkey button pops on time, and my brother Dan carves while Mum and I scramble the gravy, grind the cranberry/orange relish, and rush the squash, potatoes, peas, wine, creamed onions, and those acrid-smelling turnips onto the table. Aunt Connie sets out her masterpieces near the boys, sweet cornbread and soft banana bread: the first to be grabbed after Grace. A feast later, the dishwasher hums as we sip coffee, savor apple and pumpkin pie, and flop on couches and recliners, utterly sated, some of us snoring.

JANUARY

After our traditional, jubilant, tag-team Christmas events, which we get to string out this year by visiting each extended family for a full week, we force in a little more culture by pulling the boys to the Butler Institute of American Art in Jeff's birthplace, Youngstown, Ohio. It provides a great field trip. Once there and whined out, the boys rather enjoy the art. Could it be the Negro Baseball League images so poignantly rendered by Dean Richardson that turn their heads? They sure turn mine.

At last Jeff's parents take us to Cleveland, where we catch a flight to Salt Lake City to begin our three-week ski trip out west. The biggest homeschooling project we've shared begins to come to fruition, and we wriggle with excitement over the intrinsic rewards we anticipate for doing our homework. With backpacks and rolling pilot's luggage, we pretty easily manage clothes, boots, and skis through two airports and finally onto the Ford Ranger owned by the caretaker of the Silver Fork Lodge. There we stay for five wondrous, blizzard-filled days in Utah. The lodge offers a cozy, western refuge with firm, quilted beds and cowboy motifs everywhere, even on the shower curtain. While there, we repeatedly enjoy frosty root beer in glass mugs in the shape of cowboy boots. I splurge on four of them to send home as a keepsake, betting we'll never have root beer floats in any other glass.

Our first day out west, we ski the summit from Honeycomb Canyon at Solitude Ski Area. We feel like we're flying; though I admit I take a terribly graceless, face-plant plunge into the snow while trying to maneuver a small, rocky cliff. What a workout! All morning long, Jeff and I cruise across the mountain, praying that we won't have to ski extreme off any steep cliffs. Of course, the boys hope that we will. Where do they get all that energy? We all quit in the early afternoon to avoid jet lag and altitude adjustment problems and snuggle into the Silver Fork Lodge living room to watch a movie. Soon Tim charges back outside in all his ski gear to lunge up and then to ski down the roof-high snow mound at the end of the driveway. That kid finds fun anywhere!

More snow falls for him to work with over the weekend, two inches each hour. At Brighton, the other ski area on this craggy, canyon road, we exert our legs mercilessly to turn our skis through thick, knee-deep powder that's fluffy and fun to fall in. We don't really fall so much as lean back into a cloud now and then – a needed break. After a full day, Matt, Jeff, and I rest with our books in the sauna and eat steaks heartily in the lodge restaurant. Meanwhile, Tim lingers outside again doing flips off the sundeck into six feet of billowy powder. Watching him as we eat by the warm fire, we are well entertained. Matt's maturity shows but so does his desire to join in.

The next day, straddling the adult world and childhood, Matt cannot resist joining Tim in his new sport when avalanches close the pass and the ski areas. We are snowbound. All morning, we hear explosions as ski patrols try to dislodge unstable snow with dynamite. We listen to reports that several people have to be rescued from their cars when a snow slide lands in the parking lot at the Alta Ski Area across the canyon. It traps hundreds of skiers in the main lodge for the night. One man, buried under snow, is located by a retired, narcotics-sniffing police dog, that now lives at the ski area for just such emergencies. Two very experienced backcountry skiers armed with location devices are not so fortunate. They are found too late, still in their sleeping bags and swept far from their campsite in the night. The news makes it to New England and my parents call to make sure of our safety and to discuss the Patriots' run for the Superbowl.

Finally, the blizzard passes, and more than safe, we enjoy the advantages of our location above the pass. We find ourselves nearly alone on the mountain when the ski areas reopen, our own personal resort. In the mid-afternoon, the wind blows in blue sky and rays of sun that glisten off of every slope of the snow-locked canyon. What a sight! Looking down into the canyon, the trees are so sparse, barely interrupting the ride downhill. The boys can go anywhere, and we can see them below as we take a gentler tack. So free, we fly all over the mountain, unimpeded by trails, traffic, or trials.

A nod to homeschooling, thus far set aside for our trip, we spend a day exploring Salt Lake City and touring the Mormon Temple Square before heading to Colorado. The boys are astonished that we cannot go into the temple, and more so to learn that even if I was Mormon, I could not go in with them because of my gender. Instead, the boys conduct a fruitless ancestral search, surprising because we know this is the most renowned place to do it. We then view *Legacy*, a moving and beautifully crafted film that gives a good picture of life during the westward expansion and the travails of the Mormon pioneers. However, it gives a rose-colored view of the church, I suspect, and leads us into illuminating discussions of propaganda and church doctrine. After a day, we feel we have seen much of what Salt Lake City has to offer and prepare to move on.

Move on, we have! At 5:30 AM we finally board the train that will take us on the next leg of our journey, through the Rocky Mountains of Colorado. Unfortunately, I, in an ultra-cautious frame of mind, hustle us to the station at 3:30 AM. Mercifully, the conductor encourages us to climb aboard and to sleep across two seats each. By the time we awake it is an easy ride to Glenwood Springs, Colorado. Between sharing our camera, Matt reading Michael Crichton aloud, and games of Yahtzee, the eight-hour trip is unexpectedly full. The dome car provides a magnificent view with ruddy western scenes. Each mountain pass resembles a layered sand art display aglow in reds and yellows cut over a century ago for our chugging train and towering above a glistening river. We discover a glass house built in a cave – prairie dogs, elk, and a bald eagle standing possessively atop a frozen, sixteen-pointed buck that fell through the ice a lifetime ago. The handful of towns we pass through seemed deserted with low rustic buildings in need of paint. One resembles a modern ghost town replete with tumbleweeds tossing through the streets.

Thus, the sight of Glenwood Springs, an oasis of civilization, thrills us. The quaint train station, built of sand-colored brick with stately quoins and large windows, sits near the famous Hotel Colorado, which overlooks the elegant and expansive hot springs pool for which the town was named. Jeff, always impressing me with his encyclopedic knowledge of history, explains how the hotel's early fame attracted Theodore Roosevelt to give a speech from its main balcony. We imagine him standing there now, commanding a crowd unaccustomed to presidential visits, and sharing with them his love for the natural wonders of this land. Earlier still, Wyatt Earp's sidekick at the infamous shoot out at the O.K. Corral, Doc Holliday, hoped the springs would cure his tuberculosis. But he died at the hotel instead, when the sulfuric steam ironically hastened the weakening of his lungs. The town's lore enchants us all.

Undaunted by Holliday's misfortune, we spend the afternoon soaking in the hot springs – bubbling and crusty-white with minerals. So much steam engulfs us that I can hardly see Matt and Tim as they flip and fly off the diving board. The boys exclaim that the pool, two blocks long, is designed in the shape of a coffin. An added, eerie thrill!

Glenwood Springs wins our contest for the most charming and interesting town we have visited to date. Excellent shopping and diversion await us along its many Victorian blocks of boutiques and southwestern restaurants. Tim and I each find new winter jackets on sale and Matt finds a fabric store selling Polartec fabric lined with wind-stop nylon, which he begs me to make into a jacket for mountain biking. Who can resist such a project, especially during this, my year for projects? Both boys wear the sweaters I had time to knit them for Christmas; both have learned to knit with me, too. Tim, left-handed, created a mantra to remember the steps at just about the time we were reading about the Pirates of the Caribbean ride at Disneyworld. "Stab it, choke it, knock it off the plank!" He seems able to do most anything with his hands and his feet!

Warmed and rested, we spend the next day at Ski Sunlight, aptly named. A picnic table at the top of the mountain affords us a perfect spot to set the self-timer on the camera and take a family photo. What a festooned family we make in our bright ski duds set against an azure sky, white snow, and a bank of pine-studded mountains in the distance! Thank goodness we catch the image. The boys will never relinquish their ski time for another shot, and yet I think they will be glad for this memento for generations. Besides, we need a picture to send out for – oops missed Christmas – for Valentine's Day, I guess.

On the train to Denver the next day, we enjoy an ever-startling spectacle of unfamiliar wildlife, sunset vistas, and sedimentary-rock mountains notched for the passage of our locomotive. What a way for the boys to experience their country. Leaning back against Jeff in the dome car, I look up from my book to share in each of his alert reactions to the scene. Next to us, Tim flips through a ski magazine and arrests Matt's reading of Crichton's *Lost World* for regular updates on the gory story. Generously, Matt reads him the most gruesome parts with the intonations of an experienced radio storyteller. In the right place with the right people, we feel no rush to arrive. We already have.

In Denver, more family. Marta's son Nat, a childhood friend of mine, meets us at the station and takes us to spend a day with him, his new wife, and eight-year-old stepson. The boys enjoy a run to an arcade so much that Nat, Jane, and Russell decide to follow us to our condominium in the ski country of Summit County and join us on the slopes the following day. With Matt to baby-sit, the two couples get to slip out for margaritas and Mexican food and to find that we have much in common. Their warm and jovial company adds to the fun of a new mountain to conquer the next day, but we all have to adjust to managing a larger group. More waiting, more deciding, the routine we have developed as a foursome of skiers is disrupted, and we soon miss it. We all get so tied to our routines, even on this – our year away from the ordinary.

The next day is all ours. Familiar now with the North Peak at Keystone, we ski it all day, feeling like experts. How lucky we are to do what we love most with the people we most love. Jeff and I enjoy the soft, groomed slope of "Mozart," as mellifluous to ski as its name implies. Meanwhile, the boys bomb down "Last Alamo," explosive with moguls and fast drops. These both empty out to the same lift so that we can meet after each run and reassure my mother's heart. Someone once said that having children is like having your heart walk around outside of your body. It surely is on these mountains. And my dear hearts are soaring!

We don't last long the next day at Arapahoe Basin. The highest ski area in Summit County has been whited-out by a cloud and snow showers. While I stay with Tim on one powdery mogul run that charitably has a groomed run next to it for the less agile mom,

Jeff joins Matt to brave "The Basin." A solid skier who floats down the roughest terrain as smoothly and steadily as a track star running hurdles, Matt somehow still catches his ski in a clump of thick snow, and, not being able to see below his knees or beyond his outstretched arms in the powder, he tumbles. Ultimately, he recovers all his gear, washed off him by a bouncing, bubble bath of snow. A yard sale, they call it, when all of his equipment, skis, and poles are strewn across the trail. Returning to the lodge, he looks miserably cold and worn out with shards of ice sprinkled white on his hot pink face. He only lets me stroke away one large scab of snow from his ear. Then he collapses into a rickety metal chair that seems all too familiar with tired teenagers flopping into it. Glad to have just made myself cocoa, I hand it to him; he needs it more.

Undaunted, we make the short hop to Breckenridge Ski Area. Just below the clouds and snow, but not below the wind, it is exposed, and it is expansive. With ten peaks to choose from, our only problem is one of consensus. Excited to get to watch the American freestyle team practice on a frightening, double-black-diamond rated slope, Tim perhaps thinks he is watching his future. "I can do that!" he volunteers as he witnesses the more basic jumps. Matt rolls his eyes, as only a big brother can, eager to move on and to plummet down some steep slopes, but we take the time to fuel Tim's newfound passion. We wonder out loud which jumps Tim wants to learn when we return to Plymouth and his freestyle team.

After skiing until dusk, we then enjoy an evening stroll around the town of Breckenridge. With its backdrop of frosty mountains and open, star-sprinkled skies, Main Street invites us. We cross the charming little bridge to the town, beneath a beacon moon. Each Victorian storefront is tastefully decorated and warmly lit from within, no neon glares here. I allow myself to be drawn in, and I long to linger. Against my Puritan nature, I spend too much money. We even duck into a chocolate shop and buy Frisbee-sized cookies with chocolate chips still dripping from the oven. Decadent.

One day we ski the high life, literally and figuratively. Though we stand determined to dislike Vail for its fame and ostentation, it threatens to become our favorite resort. At lunchtime, our brought from home carrots, crackers, and powdered soup are tucked away in our locker miles away, and only confused expressions meet us when we ask where we can obtain boiling water for the packets of cocoa we always carry in our chest pockets when we ski. So, in the spirit of "When in Rome…" we brave the Two Elks Lodge for a full-pay munch. Cynically foregoing the ten-dollar hamburgers, we share huge brownies and rich cocoa. The massive, fully carpeted room is restful, in spite of three hundred American and European skiers in clunky boots. A bit catty, we determine that all the prettiest and priciest skiwear belongs to the least skilled skiers, while Handel plays softly over the loudspeakers, soothing our savagery. The ladies' room smells sweet with potpourri and fifteen full boxes of tissues that lie in wait in a tiled trough along two mirrored walls above fifteen pristine sinks. The elegance of a restaurant can always be measured by the elegance of its ladies' room. But I never thought I'd encounter such at a sporty ski resort.

On our way back to the main lodge, the boys lead us to a crest with only double-black-diamond runs to the bottom. They choose

Joy is a net of love by which you can catch souls.

- Mother Theresa

the most frightening, a two-tiered mogul run. I try to pass, but at my rescue Jeff grins boyishly and says, "Come on, we can do this!" leading me to Robert's Run, a finely groomed, smooth, double-black-diamond trail. It drops at what looks like an eighty-degree angle, a dizzying pitch. However, the fastidious grooming at Vail makes the snow feel like velvet, easy to turn through. I determine that at the least I can make one or two turns then just walk down, if I don't topple and fall all the way. I don't. After a few tentative slides, we zip down vengefully and giggle like teenagers. At the flat, we stop to look back up and admire our courage and growing expertise. Now this is exhilarating! Jeff's strong face beams, reflecting my own. We rejoin our boys, also beaming, and a white net of flurries settles on our shoulders.

We have an intimate family reunion back in Denver with my cousins, Mark and Christy, and their dog, Geronimo. He quickly becomes a favorite with the boys who listen intently to stories of how he skydived with Mark in the marines during Operation Desert Storm, making them both heroes of ours. After sticky, sweet ribs and brisk beer at a charming local diner, we hug at the station and board the train for a daunting, twenty-five hour trip to Toledo, Ohio. This time we spring for a stateroom. It's cozy. With windows on both sides, Matt and I prefer to stay there and read. Tim and Jeff stick with the dome car and hold our seats until the movie starts in the evening. The motion of the train and the surprising comfort of the drop-down beds keep us asleep all the way across Nebraska and well into the morning. The French toast, a family favorite, tastes warm and syrupy in the club car. All in all, we have a wonderful taste of train travel. It delivers us home to Jeff's parents' home rested and enlightened and in time for the Patriots' Super Bowl. The next morning, I lie in a familiar bed, not quite yet conscious or aware of my surroundings, and I erroneously wonder why the train has stopped.

On our return to New England, we stop in Connecticut where Tim has an interview at Watkinson School. Already I know we have asked too much of him. First, he can't really imagine going back to school with the problems he's encountered in the past. Second, he can't imagine going to this independent day school, so different from the public school at the other end of town. Third, and most immediately problematic, he is exhausted and happy to get out of the car, but characteristically nervous and reluctant to meet new adults. Who wants to get into a school at age ten, especially with his memories? But we hope, we pray, we promise, that this school might be different. He heads up for his interview and, gulp, to write his admissions essay with a small, serious, young admissions officer. Meanwhile we anxiously sit in the waiting room reading about this vibrant, Coalition School that, following Ted Sizer's model, focuses on teachers as coaches, democratic processes, and best of all, mastery projects in lieu of the memorization based tests of many schools. Always battling memory problems, Tim is a project guy. He is not an interview guy, however, especially not after hours in the car. When he returns, I don't sense any spark from his interviewer. With people who get Tim, there's an unmistakable spark.

The kids are sleeping soundly in the car as Jeff and I discuss our quandary. If Tim doesn't get into Watkinson, where will he go? What school will embrace him, his talents, his intelligences, and his foibles? He's gotten lost in the small neighborhood elementary schools in Windsor; how will he ever survive in the huge middle school crowded with twelve hundred kids? And if he does get into the school, how will we afford it? Will he receive a scholarship like Matt, or will we have to sell our house? How lucky that, living on campus, we can. But to do so would be to give up all the equity we have. Then how will we buy a home whenever we leave Loomis or retire? Jeff doesn't look around corners as nervously as I do. One day at a time.

FEBRUARY

Back in New Hampshire, our new home awaits us on our return and with it a new project. Delighted that the new house is in town where they hope to see more of their friends, the boys are nevertheless disgruntled, as we are. The house feels shabby and dirty, a disappointment after our pristine, high-ceilinged home on the mountain. Still, on the main drag in Plymouth, this one is accessible, regardless of the weather. We'll just have to get to work homemaking.

First, we remove and bag up all the dusty curtains and linens, and go out to ski for a day while our realtor finally calls in a cleaning squad. We return physically spent and relieved to find a clean, shabby home with bare windows and beds. Hustling to unpack just our necessities and make beds, we realize that homeschooling is going to have to wait. Settling in takes priority, and from what we can see, it's going to take some time and considerable effort.

February in New Hampshire does not drag on as one may presume, too much to do. It worries me that we find little time or discipline for homeschooling. And added to that, we packed everything up so quickly that it is daunting to set up our school again. Daunting and seemingly, perhaps, unnecessary. The boys have become such self-determined learners. They fill their mornings with fascinating discussions, readings, and forages through our local library, just a few blocks away. They have already met the goals we set for them. Tim appears to be reading on grade level, though slowly and with spotty memory, and Matt's SSAT scores came in so high that he stunned our colleague when she interviewed him at Loomis. We can relax, confident that their academic skills are well intact.

Thus, sandwiched between our January trip out west and a March trip down south, February provides a respite with opportunities to get out of our dark, musty house and ski nearly every afternoon. Preparing for his first freestyle competition, Tim skis for nine days in a row, running up and down one mogul run, repeatedly. Jeff accompanies him, skiing along the side of the run, while Matt and I explore the mountain and its smoother trails. Considering Howard Gardner's theory of multiple intelligences, we recognize that Tim's weaknesses in basic linguistic and computational realms receive less instructional attention lately, while his strengths in kinesthetic, spatial, and interpersonal intelligence receive constant, self-imposed challenge and practice. Free to be, he literally runs with his strengths, paying relentless attention to detail and developing confidence and resilience. We hope that these skills will serve him well later when applied to traditional academic pursuits as well. Matt stays home with me on Tuesdays and Thursdays to rest before his basketball games with the Holderness middle school team. During that time, he exercises his strengths in linguistic and musical intelligence, reading voraciously while listening to his growing collection of compact discs. Dumas' *The Count of Monte Cristo* holds his imagination this month as much as Michael Crichton did all the way across the country. His love of reading makes him a great conversationalist.

I must abandon the family and any hope of homeschooling most mornings, having taken on more students this month, to help pay our skyrocketing heat and electricity bills. When my men are not skiing, I return home each afternoon to find the house cleaner and more moved into. Jeff seems to enjoy surprising me and sets daily goals, to have the bathroom walls washed or all the kitchen cabinets all scrubbed, before I return. It looks so fresh and clean I assume that he's been painting! No wonder so many men want an old-fashioned housewife. It is marvelous to come home and find the extra housework that has been nagging at me all done. We find our home cleaner and more inviting each day.

The boys like it too. They begin to invite friends over, and the friends come in droves. Few ever made it up the mountain to our other house, but here Matt and Tim delight in being close to the hub of town life. With the middle school just across the street, a gang of boys drops by on their way home from school each day. I make sure the woodstove is stoked and there are cookies or fresh bread cooling on the rack, waiting for hungry guys. One night, Jeff makes ribs and pizza for a bunch of the kids he coached in football and who Matt keeps close.

"Can I go to the middle school in the spring? We're not really homeschooling anymore, and I want to be with my friends." Matt drops into the conversation that night. He's right, at least in terms of traditional textbook work, the structure he equates with learning, our homeschool has waned. But with drive, intelligence, and wonder, the boys are exploring every day. They are natural sponges for new learning, relentless in the pursuit. We know that Matt wants to get back into "school mode" before attending Loomis Chaffee next fall. We suspect he also wants to get to know some of the girls the boys all talk about and to be in the center of the social whirl, which, he has learned, happens in school.

For Valentine's Day Jeff takes me out to dinner to my favorite restaurant, The Common Man, where we enjoy wine and cheese and steak or halibut and garlic mashed potatoes, all of our favorite foods. We talk about the boys, take stock of the year, and plan for the spring. We look forward to going on Jeff's annual trip to The Draper

Baseball School in Florida together, for three weeks rather than just one this year. Appreciating his coaching expertise, the Drapers have asked Jeff to stay and instruct for as long as he can. Our trip south offers an opportunity to visit dear friends in Philadelphia and in Washington, D.C. where Valley Forge and national museums await our boys. It will be a great expedition.

But what of when we return? Matt's request to go to school provides a timely opportunity to get the boys back in the swing as students, to prepare Matt for Loomis Chaffee and to reassure Watkinson School that Tim can achieve in the classroom. We now know what Tim can do from the strides he's made with us, from his interest in reading anything related to camping, skiing, or building, and from his willingness to complete his applications with care, "just to give yourself options next year," we tell him. But the people at Watkinson don't know. Understandably, they are reluctant to accept a parent's evaluation of a child's abilities, especially after receiving his grades and recommendations from his last elementary school which indicated his struggles last spring. Seems so long ago to us, but the admissions office wants to know more. One of Ted Sizer's Essential Schools, thankfully they are convinced that intelligent students with learning disabilities, like Einstein and Edison, can achieve greatness, and they are intrigued by our commitment to taking Tim out of school for a year and teaching him ourselves. They see the possibility. But have we realized it? Have we spent too much time skiing and moving and homemaking at the expense of real growth in Tim's abilities? A spring term at the Plymouth Middle School would certainly let us and Watkinson and, most importantly, Tim, know. We put our heads together and consider the crux, his school anxiety. How will we ever get him to go?

In the morning I slip out from under the soft weight of a down comforter and prance across the icy floor to grab my slippers and a big sweater. Stuffing paper into the wood stove downstairs, I rue the fact that I have to go out to the shed for wood. Another light snow has fallen, leaving the yard crystal-glazed and glimmering in the early sunlight. By the time the fire sparks and crackles enough to heat the space around me, my tea boils and warms me from inside. How I'd love to crank the oil heat. But the housing stipend from Loomis just covers our rent and electrical bills; the most critical lessons of the winter have been to remember to turn off the lights and to stoke the fire. I slink by boxes of books and lesson plans, left untouched and unlikely to be used anytime soon. We're still moving in, skiing as a family, and planning our next adventure.

Homeschool lessons have been rather amorphous this month. After our trip, the boys did some journal writing and polished off their school applications. Matt applied to Holderness and Loomis, but never did send in his application to Phillips Exeter. Still, the process of visiting and interviewing was invaluable, giving him a sense of choice, control and commitment. Did he decide that he didn't want to leave home after all, or did he just quit writing the essay? Tim applied to Watkinson and Kingswood Oxford, struggling over the essays, which came out clear, heartfelt, and mechanically flawed – a good representation of his writing ability. Matt will go where we go, probably back to Loomis, or possibly staying here, and Tim, we'll have to see. I hope he can attend one of the private middle schools in our area of Connecticut. I don't see how he can succeed at Windsor's public middle school with its crowded classrooms and its limited support for bright students with learning problems.

And what will I do? I don't want to return to teaching in the public schools. I'm burned out or spoiled by the pedagogical freedom I've enjoyed in private settings this year. Why can't we just stay here? I love my work and our new community, so warm and down to earth compared to my busy peers in the suburbs. Back home there is a tempting job opening for a director of the Learning Skills Program at Watkinson, but that would be tough on Tim. Besides, it's what I am doing now that I love. As an independent learning specialist, I am freed from paperwork, I get to focus on my students and their individual needs. How can I continue working one-on-one with college bound students who struggle in school? Our plans for next year are as nebulous as our plans for the sabbatical were at this time a year ago. Jeff should return, it is the tradition, and he is a traditionalist, but he doesn't absolutely have to, I plead. Matt always assumed he would go to Loomis, but he could do as well here at Holderness. I will do whatever best serves my family. But who knows what's best for Tim? Thinking really creatively, I even wonder if I should teach the disabled skiers at Mount Snow, so that Tim can ski on their freestyle team next year while attending their small, private skier's school. It's a radical idea, but he is so passionate about skiing, and passions matter. And he would benefit from a small, individualized school setting. Can we create the right life for all of us? So far, the sabbatical has worked out well for each of us step by stumbling step, so I guess this is another time when I cannot orchestrate an ideal future. I'll just have to be patient about what is to come next year too.

Jeff is busy carting the kids around with their friends, and I am glad. I am seeing so many students now that I'm not available for much carpooling during the day. Thank goodness I am busy though; we need the extra income. And I find I need Holderness School. I love having lunch with colleagues, worrying together over curriculum and kids. I wonder whether I might be needed to teach here next year. It seems that there will be an English opening. If Tim has to go to public school, I'd rather he attend the small middle school here in town where class sizes are reasonable and the faculty know all the students quite well. I know Jeff would love to teach and coach at Holderness as well. He hasn't sent his contract to Loomis Chaffee yet, so I am hopeful, feeling at home for the first time in years. Raised in a small town, I am not a suburban girl, but Loomis is such a good match for Matt, academically and on the baseball field. We'll just have to see how we fit the pieces together to build our new life, again.

MARCH

My March break frees us to travel again, this time along the Eastern Seaboard. We pack the floor of the minivan so that our Golden Retriever, Brittany, and occasionally the kids, can stretch out and sleep on top of our bags and baseball equipment. A good stop over on the way down to Florida, Philadelphia offers us a chance to stay with Laura and Steve, dear friends of ours who recently moved there from Simsbury, Connecticut. Their children have long been great friends with ours, and with four of them, life is always bustling at their house. Laura loves the idea of homeschooling and wants to have her kids share in our experience while we are there, so we all visit Valley Forge. It offers a fascinating field trip. We view an informative videotape at the visitors' center and then begin to walk through light showers to the original buildings. It quickly becomes clear that with the buildings spread out in their original positions, and without the horses that George Washington and his colleagues rode, we would need a car, dampening the historical effect.

In each dark and stifling cabin, the kids study how the soldiers must have made their rough shelters and wonder at having to share them with eleven other men through that brutal winter. They inspect the walls and determine that the cold, mud packing had been lately replaced by modern concrete. General Washington's quarters, a sturdy stone house by the river that was donated for his use by a Tory family, stands quaint and remarkably small when one considers how many officers and aides had to live there with the general and his wife. We hear how they had to sleep in the hallways as well as the living and dining rooms and how Martha made the General's bedroom into a meeting place for the French ambassador and other foreign dignitaries as needed. In this way she made do with very little to help convince the European allies that America could survive as an independent country. Our foremothers' stories catch my imagination. How effectively they brought people together, so that others, often men, could lead them forward together.

It well follows that we should visit the results of her efforts in Washington the following week. We stay with my best friend Cath and her family, and visit the Washington, Jefferson, and Lincoln Memorials, the Smithsonian, the Holocaust Museum, and the newly erected, expansive, black wall memorializing the soldiers who died in Vietnam. Fascinated, Matthew has read many books and novels about the war this year as the focus of his I-search for social studies. Tim O'Brien's *The Things They Carried* has riveted us all as our read-aloud.

Breathlessly, we locate the name of the father of a boy Jeff played little league with. His service has been memorialized here as it was in Jeff's hometown. Jeff shares his memory of how his whole team was stunned and aggrieved when one of their fathers died in the war. He recalls how a new field was built and named in his honor. I sense how it all became part of the hushed sanctity that baseball fields hold for my husband.

Jeff thrives in his element. Each day in Florida, he suits up in his new baseball uniform and joins the Draper brothers to instruct seventy boys in their favorite pastime. Matt and Tim drink in the instruction, especially when it comes from these famous, retired major leaguers. The Drapers embrace my family, and I stand by, grateful. One day Duane, who played for my own dear Red Sox, stands beside me watching all three of my young men and muses, "Susan, you are a woman many times blessed." I swallow, not knowing how to respond. Does he sense my discomfort on the sidelines, away from work and friends? Am I immodest to agree? We watch and smile as Matt pokes Tim with a bat as he jogs by and as Jeff gathers boys to him like the Pied Piper. I smile, nodding. "Many times."

Each day of baseball camp begins with an optional chapel talk in right field, a perfect expression of Jeff's favorite adage from Wes Westrum. "Baseball is like church, many attend, but few understand." Congregational Church members, but not regular churchgoers, we find this setting far more conducive to our boys meeting God. They always choose to attend the daily chapel. One day, Blake delivers what becomes my favorite talk. He shares that he has learned that to follow

Christ is to search for the good in all that you do, quoting Proverbs 23:7, "As a man thinketh in his heart, so is he." For the boys he interprets that when a player imagines success and plays his hardest for it, inevitably, his bat will send the ball flying, because the Spirit, or Grace, has gone through the player. What a passionate way to express his pursuit of excellence, a pursuit that I hope the boys will share on the baseball field.

On Tim's birthday, I spend the morning collecting cake, paper goods, and presents. It rains, so ball players of all ages cram into our crowded motel room, munching cake and congratulating Tim with cheers and boyish birthday slugs. Camp owner, Hank Draper flops down on the edge of the bed and gives Tim a major league birthday hug. Fellow shortstops, he and Tim connected from the first. And, of course, Tim is starstruck by this icon, the leading hitter of the 1978 World Series, even though he played for the Yankees, any Red Sox fan's nemesis. Despite being a damp, cramped hotel room party, it becomes one of Tim's most memorable as Hank lets him try on his World Series ring.

Jeff's parents and his sister, Lauren's, family come down to visit for a few days, bringing Tim presents and bringing me their video camera. It gives me the sense of purpose I need in this man's world. I spend the remainder of our time at the camp creating training tapes so that we can take the Draper's fabulous instructions and locker room stories home with us. Lauren brings her newly adopted daughter, Grace Tundee, for her first visit to Disney World, and we get to tag along for some wonderful outings. The Magic Kingdom offers fresh splendor as we see it through the eyes of a little girl who, at one point in her three years, saw nothing but the walls of her room in a Romanian orphanage. No wonder her eyes get as big as her smile at the sight of Mickey Mouse, the Pirates of the Caribbean ride, my favorite since childhood, and the dancing dolls on the It's a Small World ride.

Epcot is worth a second visit. I can't say the same for any other attractions in central Florida, though they are all fun once. I doubt the boys agree; they find Epcot diverting but slow moving. Jeff and I would love to go back without them so that we could enjoy foreign dining and entertainment without having to spend endless hours with the boys in the display room full of new computer games and inventions.

At night, at a major league preseason baseball game, Kenny Lofton and Bob Feller sign Tim's official American League balls, bringing his total collection to twelve signed balls of some value. His greatest prize is yet to come when all three Drapers give him and Matt balls they have signed, expressly for them.

On the way back to our hotel, I awake just as we turn off the highway. At the bottom of the exit, a long red light holds us close to a desperate looking man. His thin frame and willowy hair remind me of Jon Voigt in the movie "Coming Home." He grips a sign: "Hungry. Please help." The words and his dull, blue eyes work on me like a cow works on a dry wad of hay, softening it. My awareness slowly turns to the box of saltines between Jeff and me, and in a careful, swift motion, I roll the window down just far enough to push the stack of crackers out. The man's eyes abruptly seem to focus and to ask a question. I nod. Moving as cautiously as I have, he approaches the car gently, watching for signs of danger, grasps the bag, and backs up. He clings tight to his safe frown, but his eyes, suddenly soulful, thank me. In the same short instant, Jeff's head jerks from the road to me, "What are you doing?" He whispers, quickly and defensively responding to the green light. "That was a terrible risk." He's right I know as I glance at the children safe and nourished in the back seat. I nod again, but hope that in exchange for some risk, they have witnessed compassion.

On our road trip back up the eastern seaboard from Orlando to New Hampshire, we first stop in Saint Augustine. What a charming town with its Spanish architecture, drawbridge, 17th century revolutionary fort, and long beaches. The beach, breezy and refreshing, beacons us to join a few other cars that have driven right across its hard, flat sand and parked against the grassy edge. We do, and soon we all race for the water, squealing in the joy of getting out of the hot car and into the water. Within minutes, a large crab pinches Tim, which only adds to his excitement once he knows he is okay. He and Matt boogie-board in the surf, build a sand doll and romp with our dog, Britty, who loves the sand but shies from the surf in a darting dance. We camp out near the beach, and at dawn Britty and I have the sun-soaked beach to ourselves.

A day later and a few hundred miles closer to home, Williamsburg, impressive and imposing in its historical aura, disappoints us compared to our more interactive and child-centered Sturbridge Village in Massachusetts. However, we relish an authentic, period meal in the center of the historic section and fully enjoy the history-oriented shops. The most fascinating part of the tour, we all agree, is offered at the slave quarters of a nearby plantation. The interpreters impress us with the matter-of-fact way they show us how slaves made-do in captivity, with the rudimentary cabins and small garden patches they were granted.

Although they were only allowed to plant and sow their main source of sustenance during their only free time – on Sundays. What an unjust existence, and what a resourceful and resilient people. Though impressed, I know the boys will remember the evening best, when we enjoy the recreation of a multitude of roller coasters at Busch Gardens. We go to sleep dizzy and happy to be heading home.

Spring
Commencements

April

It's the first day back to school in nearly a year, Matt's up and dressed, excited and nervous. Do I smell a little cologne? However, Tim balks. I greet him cheerfully, pretending he must not have heard me the three times I called from the kitchen already, and I pull up his shades as he tunnels deep into his warm bed. Grasping the covers like a shield, he groans through clenched teeth, "I'm not going!"

One by one, all three of us try comforting him, cajoling him, then threatening him: nothing works. Finally, I settle in beside him and tell my miserable, muttering mound, "You always react this way to the first day of anything. I have to make you go." I aim for gentle firmness. "Then, when you're grown and afraid to start a new job, you'll remember this day and how everything turned out great, and you'll get up and make yourself go." I inhale, listening. No response, so far so good. Jeff appears at the door. "Your dad and I are going to make you go now. So, all you have to decide is: do you want to walk into school yourself or should I call the principal to meet us at the car and carry you in?" I leave the room, hoping. He knows we just might, because we have done it before. When he was in second grade Jeff had to carry him to school and hand him, crying bitterly, into the arms of his teacher. Now older, wiser, and better prepared for success, this time he finally shuffles downstairs and out the door in a smart, new sweater and Tommy Hilfiger jeans, all the rage.

By now it's late, so I drive him down the short road to school. Still reluctant, he makes it to the office; then balks again. He doesn't want to walk in late, alone. The assistant principal, Marie, the mother of one of his buddies, greets Tim. So tuned in to him, she calls over one of his good friends, and the two of them trot off to their classroom together, Tim relieved to know someone and pretending everything's fine. At the end of the day I am glued to the kitchen window, facing the road to school, vigilant. He bounces in the door with two friends in tow and a big smile: the morning frights, forgotten, and my first day of school cookies, devoured.

The next day Jeff takes me out for lunch for a long-deferred adult-time treat. We celebrate our first day with no kids, no dailies, no curriculum to create. A year ago, we tried to do this regularly to be sure there were no unresolved issues we needed to discuss when we were both parenting and working long hours. Now, with the confidences we share daily while bringing in wood for the stove or working in the kitchen, lunch isn't a necessary appointment, but just a chance to spoil ourselves a little now that the boys are back in school. We talk about next year. Jeff needs to send his contract in to Loomis Chaffee, though our colleagues at Holderness and at the Plymouth Schools keep bringing up possible openings they'd like us to fill. I don't have any really compelling reasons for us to stay here, though I'd like to, and if we do go back to Connecticut, somehow, I feel sure we will be back. The sense of home we have created, perhaps we can replicate in Windsor. It'll just take diligence and faith.

We laugh, relieved at how happy the boys are to be back in the thick of the social whirl. Our house, though modest, is perfectly situated right across the street from the road to school, so at three o'clock the boys usually bolt through the door with a gang of buddies who live farther along, and I always make sure there is plenty of snack food. Enjoying school, his friends, and the routine, Matt has a new understanding of why I always say that if I ever won the lottery I would not quit working. It is why I am working now. I would miss sharing common goals and efforts shared with friends and colleagues. Now he and Tim seem similarly enthused to share school with the friends they've come to know so well through sports, church, and community activities. Having them start right where they left off last year, just completing fifth and eighth grade, has given them academic security and familiarity while providing, we hope, a smooth transition to middle and high school next fall. We chuckle, astounded at how mad Tim became last night when we said we might have to miss a day of school next week to go to Ohio for the spring vacation break. A year ago, he would have bemoaned, "Only one day?" Now he's insisting, "I can't miss school!" His teacher and he are definitely doing something right!

Tim's teacher calls to let us know how he's acclimating to school life. "Socially, it's as if he had been here all year long." Not surprising, Tim is a socialite. "And academically, he's doing fine. He needed only a quick reminder before he was able to take off with fractions. His science and social studies teachers have both remarked on how much he has to offer to class discussions, especially in social studies where they are studying the west, where he has just been." I exhale, she already knows him well. "He is in a regular reading group, and I was afraid he would struggle with the book that he chose, but he seems to be enjoying it." Grateful, I have to agree. Admittedly, I had been afraid he might pretend to read it, trying to look normal in his new school. However, when I watch him reading it at home, his eyes track the text without much of the old wanderings. Not only is he reading on grade level, his responses to questions indicate that he understands it well and feels, for the first time in his life, proud of his reading ability. He even confides in our neighbor, Maryjo: "You're not going to believe this, but I like school!"

Matt seems to be on a roll as well. His algebra teacher, and not tangentially, his baseball coach, is on his case about making careless errors and skipping steps. Since they have a dual relationship, Matt is eager to impress him and to become as disciplined about math as he is about blocking wild pitches. His best friend since we moved here a year ago is in all of his classes, so he and Johnny walk home and complete most of their homework together. When we ask if he would mind moving here permanently if his dad or I were to be offered a good teaching position at Holderness, Matt shrugs as only a cool eighth grader can. "It wouldn't be a bad thing." Now we know that this year has been a good thing for the whole family.

> *Once you see a child's self-image begin to improve, you will see significant gains in achievement areas, but even more important, you will see a child who is beginning to enjoy life more.*
>
> - Wayne Dyer

Tim makes another breakthrough as a reader on our next road trip. As we drive to Ohio for a family wedding, Jeff offers him five cents for every sign that he reads. Well, in a few hours he reads one hundred signs. Each one speeds by, forcing him to read more efficiently than he ever has. Many times, vowel blends and word endings stump him, and each of us, even Matt, takes turns coaching him through. I note that, in particular, he struggles with the endings "-tion" and "-ity" with r-controlled vowels and with vowel blends such as "ei" and "au." Most telling is his struggle with the sign "emergency and authorized vehicles only" which is posted along the median strip every few miles across Pennsylvania. It takes at least twelve repeated readings until he finally decodes the word "authorized." As the research has shown, repeated readings are powerful medicine against dyslexia.

On the way home Tim tires of straining to read the signs, and independently, for the first time ever, elects to read a chapter in his book to pass the time in the car. He asks me to time him and reads at an easy and age appropriate 150 words per minute. When he finishes, he spends several miles catching me up on what's happening to Mary Ellen, the protagonist in *Bound for Oregon* by Jean Van Luellen. Until now I thought he would never express such enthusiasm for reading!

MAY

Matt procrastinates. So do I. Why is it that we encourage our kids to grow up like us, and then we're annoyed when they do? With considerable prodding Matt finally has collected several resources for a research project on the invention of the mountain bike. Jeff has supervised his breaking the project down into manageable steps outlined in his plan book: outline, rough draft, etc. Last week, when I asked how it was going, a stern, "It's under control, Mom!" abruptly killed the conversation. Well, it was not. Now, two days before the due date, Matt's note cards are missing, his outline is skeletal at best, and his rough draft is nonexistent. My hovering only results in his writing five paragraphs that far too closely resemble one of his articles. Mercifully for him and excruciatingly for me, I have to leave for Connecticut tomorrow to scout out a new job for me and a new school for Tim to attend next year.

Jeff takes matters more lightly. "I'm sure he'll bomb," he says, acting so cool, so unperturbed, when I am frantic. "But he won't!" My voice emerges shrill and shrewish. I hate that. "He'll write a mechanically perfect paper with loads of facts and not one independent thought and get an A." It's happened too many times before. I suggest that maybe Matt should have to miss his baseball game to get it done, a mutinous idea in this family. That will certainly teach him something. But what? That his parents will punish him for procrastinating even before the assignment is overdue? That his mother browbeats his dad as well as him? I know it's a bad idea. Jeff's is better. "Look, he'll go straight home from the game and work on it. Then, if I feel that he has failed to develop a thesis or fully credit his references, he'll have to start all over. He'll learn." Needless to say, Matt stays up until midnight. The essay has a simple thesis, but it's his. "I can't wait 'til next year," Jeff smirks, proud of his colleagues at Loomis Chaffee. "He is going to get his hat handed to him." But we know that like sweet cream in a butter churn, Matt will rise to the standard eventually. I wonder, as often I have, whether my young "absent-minded professor" son has an attention deficit disorder. I am reluctant to think so. Just because I work with gifted kids with special needs, doesn't mean that both of mine have issues. Perhaps he just suffers from over-indulgent, micromanaging mother syndrome. It's a moot point anyway. If he does have an attention problem, we will just continue to teach him strategies and assure him that many in our family have learning issues combined with areas of great talent. I think of my uncle Phil Wilson, a world renowned trombonist, who struggled to learn to read, even to read music, and yet has written arrangements for Buddy Rich for a Grammy nomination and for Aretha Franklin, my favorite jazz artist next to Phil. As well as I know they work, we won't consider stimulant medications that might inhibit Matt's appetite when he's hoping to play football against brawny high school opponents next year. So, Matt will just continue to be Matt: bright, kind, athletic, insightful, and forgetful.

Before leaving town, I work with my Holderness students for the last time and give them each a personalized gingerbread man for luck. Admittedly a goofy gift, it's perfect for exam week when my students all prize comforts of home and between meal snacks more than usual, and it fits our budget. They have all had an excellent term, especially Ellie, my only senior, who has finally broken through her glass ceiling and has earned B's in two of her toughest courses. I've written her this end of the term letter to help her remember what we worked on when she starts college next fall, maybe I will share it with Matt as he begins high school next year:

Dear Ellie,

As you head into next year, I want to remind you of a few ways to take care of that creative, visual, and sometimes-scattered mind of yours.

First, you know I'm going to say it, always use a planner. Plan backwards from every long-term assignment, and don't forget to schedule in your social time so that you can play as well as study. Everything does come to those who work hard. Schedule in ski races and photo time too, they eat up time. Preview every textbook reading so that you can determine the essentials before details bog you down. Focus on key ideas and details only as they provide support.

Read. And stick with the likes of Maya Angelou. As with skiing, only practice with good equipment will improve your skill. Her new book, *Wouldn't Take Nothing for My Journey Now*, might make for good company this summer. I have a feeling you will enjoy it.

Always, always map out your ideas after a reading and before writing an essay. That brain of yours needs an external, visual representation of all its great ideas before it can prioritize and organize a strong thesis. Thread that thesis through every paragraph using related verbs, adjectives, and metaphors. Check for consistent verb tenses. Read your work aloud; you will hear your grammar, for better or for worse.

Start planning for exams in September. Keep a separate, colored sheet of paper for each course on which you jot down all the key concepts that the teacher seems to overemphasize. This will become your exam study guide in December. During exam week, remember our three-tiered approach to studying: First, spend an hour organizing and highlighting your most critical notes, tests, quizzes, and old essays. Then, the hard part, study what you have highlighted in several, determined, thirty minute bursts. Don't leave anything for cramming; that will just knock out some critical ideas that you need to keep in mind more. And finally, keep your confidence high by "roaming around the known" for twenty minutes before the exam. Start speaking the language of that course. Imagine the test and feel yourself acing it. Just as you had your disabled skiers imagine winning before their races.

Work hard at what you love. Stay healthy. Have a wonderful summer and a good start in the fall.

Fondly,

Ms. Ross

The next weekend I am off to my twentieth reunion at Phillips Exeter Academy. At the request of my classmates, I have set up four classes with our professors, so that we can all experience a Harkness discussion again, a unique learning environment that few of us have enjoyed since graduating. I bop into Professor Richards' class where we sit around the Harkness Table, oval and oak with twelve slides that pull out for test taking. Gripping the old Academy armchairs, we reacquaint ourselves with each other and with this dynamic approach to learning from one another. We hungrily dive into a discussion of Richards' finding that the key influencers of Lincoln's speeches, Edward Everett, Daniel Webster, and George Bancroft, all attended our school in the 1800s. It's no wonder that in his despair over the education his son received at home, Lincoln sent Robert to PEA to prepare for Harvard. A long-standing tradition that has led us to affectionately refer to the Academy as "Preparation H."

Happily, I find a still impressive, but less stodgy, place. As one of the first girls to be accepted, I remember it as a formidable man's world, with few women in power and few girls' sports. I failed then to convince the head of the athletic department, my father's best man Ted, to allow me to play baseball. He knew I could play, having watched me grow up with three brothers who mostly let me catch. But he wouldn't yield – a quality I found true of most of my teachers then. I credit him though, with encouraging me to become crew coxswain, instead. He knew me well; with my outspoken and competitive nature, I was chosen to steer for the boys' varsity shell, a high honor, and I continued to cox crew successfully through college. Since my day, my coaches have come to understand the inherent sexism in the distinction I enjoyed. So, given that there is a fine girls' crew as well, coxswains are now assigned by gender rather than by ability. Thus, I was the last girl on the boys' team. It made for strong bonds, though, and I am most delighted to see my oarsmen, all grown and successful – on Wall Street, in dentistry, in biotechnics, and in politics. But I miss Ted who, after losing his battle with cancer, was immortalized as the paternal coach in *The World According to Garp*, by my fellow faculty brat, John Irving. Still, it is good to see my Academy, all grown up and gentler than in the days when it coveted the questionable distinction of being the toughest prep school in the world. It remains impressive, and though I am glad Matt decided to stay home and go to Loomis Chaffee, I wouldn't blame him for wanting to enjoy the educational opportunity I barely appreciated years ago.

At our class picnic, I catch up with Andrea, one of only eight girls who spent all four years with me at PEA. We had been gymnasts together with long 70's hair and a diehard love of the Beatles. She lives in Greenwich Village. As far from my new life in the mountains as can be, and she expresses her curiosity and envy about our great escape. She asks good, probing questions about our sabbatical, and, as a writer and editor for a theater review magazine, she asks if I've thought of writing about it. Well, yes, actually, but it's only a journal, and I'm completely daunted by the prospect of trying to get it published. A book I once wrote for siblings of children with disabilities was shot down years ago with kind notes about my writing style but no tangible encouragement. Well, she wants to see this anyway, so I'll touch it up madly to send to her within the month. I leave PEA inspired, but whoever doesn't? On my way out of Exeter, I enroll in the University of New Hampshire's summer writing workshop to help induce me to finish my book with style and to start to work on my sixth year degree in secondary school education. The latter, I hope, will help prepare me for training teachers at the college level, a step I would love to take, in order to affect the lives of more children with special needs.

Matt's all set to attend Loomis, and we are so pleased. It's a good match for him academically and athletically, and we are eager to keep him close. Can't get closer than the school where we live. Finding the right match for Tim is a conundrum. I need to visit prospective schools for him, so I'm spending three days in Connecticut. In the course of my visits I am taken with Watkinson School where small, interactive classes and a focus on mastery projects are its hallmark. Tim is a project man. Scripting the lessons in three of its classrooms and five of the classrooms at our town's middle school, I keep a tally every five minutes to see how many students are on task, the primary measure of effective learning. I find that almost all of the ten students in Watkinson's small classes are attentive, while only about half of the twenty-four students in our local school's classes show interest in the lessons at any given time. Class size, as ever, is the key to students' success. So, we will have to find a way to afford the private school: a daunting expense, especially after a year living on one income. If we must, we can sell our house and continue to live on campus at Loomis.

I set out to find a job for next year, but instead I find my niche. The Loomis Chaffee administration is not only eager for Jeff's return, but the director of academic support services needs me to work with their students who struggle. In addition, the director of consulting at the Capitol Region Education Council asks me to conduct several in-service workshops for faculty in Connecticut's public schools starting in August. Both provide a chance to effect real change in the lives of students with special needs, the opportunities sound tempting but unlikely to create a full-time demand. So, on a lark, I visit my graduate school, Saint Joseph College, and put my name in for a position as an adjunct faculty member in the Education Department. Fingers crossed, that will fill my plate for next year, and I return home to New Hampshire. Happy with our plans for the fall but wistful about leaving, I dedicate myself to our last season up north.

I wish I had better follow through. I'm sure every parent does, but this time Tim really paid for it. Yesterday, when he bombed around the yard with friends and root beer after school, I heard glass break.

Inside and focused on getting the laundry done, I called down to them and asked what had broken. "Don't worry mom," he reassured me, "We'll clean it up."

"Good," I responded in a firm voice that resembled my mother's, "because you guys will be running around barefoot soon, and I don't want anyone getting hurt."

Now it's the next day, and Tim hobbles into the house after a rousing water gun match whimpering, "Don't freak out mom." I am puzzled, but not for long. Apparently Tim has slid into the same broken root beer bottle and cut his knee. It was never picked up. With no time for recriminations, I sit him on the edge of the tub with his leg up while I inspect and clean the wound, apply pressure, and call over my shoulder for Jeff to get the butterfly bandages. Matt, always anticipating me, silently grabs the trash basket and gloves and heads outside to pick up the glass. As I clean the cut with hydrogen peroxide, Tim's face tightens. I pause to stroke his hair and catch his tears, slowly rolling and threatening to drop, wet and itchy, down his neck. I remind him to breathe and to pretend that he's floating on the raft at the lake listening to the loons. As I dress the cut, I hope he doesn't feel my hands shaking with stored adrenaline. Rather, Tim watches the process, fascinated. Jeff can't look but soon sets us up with cocoa and cookies for a quiet, read-aloud evening. Finally, after the boys are asleep, tucked in under soft, cotton sheets, I slump against Jeff and exhale.

Matt claims to hate poetry. But he seems to have a flair for it. In general, he writes with a clear and sophisticated style, but he has always regarded writing as his weakness. It's not. He's a born communicator. But finally, he is starting to see himself as a good writer. Confidence is everything. Last week, after Matt had thrown away all his old homework, which included several poems that I wanted to keep, his English teacher sent home a copy that he had kept for his files. I am so grateful to have it:

Good Day
As the wind blows through my car window,
I can smell the ocean.
It's the crisp, salty smell
Of good times and good weather.
The sun gleams down on me
As I glide through traffic.
Every light turns green
And the white blanket of sand
Shimmers in the tropical sun.
I think it's going to be a good day.

Matthew Brooks Ross

Driving is such a rite of passage in our country, and Matt cannot wait. Only a year away from getting his license, Matt obviously equates it with freedom, independence and hope. He seems to connect Florida with those feelings too, the place where he dreams of being free to play baseball all year long. I am grateful to have this nugget of Matt's passions, this embryo of his self-expression and sense of self. Watching my young man sleeping, growing before my eyes, I see his high brow, set off by a chestnut cowlick, his soft, pink pout, unchanged since his first days in our lives, and I see more. Whenever the scar on Matt's chin catches my eye, I feel that pinch of regret. I see it this morning, when I slip in to cover him up at dawn. The covers have fallen in a tangle on the floor with his wet bathing suit, grungy baseball uniform that he superstitiously won't wash until the end of the tournament, and linen sweater that I devoted two months to knitting for him this winter. In late May, it's again on the floor, ready to wear. Barely audible, he mumbles "Thanks Mom," and curls up in the warmth I tuck around him, and the scar catches my eye again, cruelly reminding me that I wasn't there.

Five years ago, I had just returned to teaching full time and was at work all day for the first time in his young life. He was a competitive eight-year-old and fell hard on the gym floor during an all-out basketball game that other kids thought was just another gym class. For the first time, Jeff was called first, and though he had to scrounge a car from a fellow coach, he flew to school and had Matt at the doctor's office within twenty minutes. He tells me he was fine until the needle pierced Matt's soft freckled skin, bending it in, popping it crimson. Matt didn't flinch, but Jeff's stomach did, and he had to step away from the smell of alcohol and Novocaine to breathe air less acrid. So obsessed with motherhood, I always found it hard to relinquish the boys to Jeff's gentle care. It's hard for me now, preparing to relinquish them to their own care. Hard, but critical. I write:

Matt-a-tat
I lie in my bed,
                              shivering
          and hardly hear
          my mother coming,
          just beyond sleep.
Then wool blankets fly
          and nestle over me
          with her warm smoothing
          of my fresh
                    shorn
                              hair.
She tucks me in, tightly,
          "like an envelope,"
                    I murmur.
And her kiss falls,
          on my forehead
          petal-like,
                    softly,
                              sealing me,
so that I barely stir.

JUNE

This morning Tim dragged himself from bed for an early ballgame complaining, "We can't beat these guys anyway." Now at the game he stands off third base, feet shifting anxiously. After he blithely steals the base on an overthrow, the pitcher watches him, wary, knowing he has wheels. Tim shouts encouragement to his teammate at the plate in that rusty, little league monotone, "C'mon Jesse, knock it out there, you got him, Jes." Leaning from the base, he taunts the pitcher, hoping to rattle him into the overthrow that will send Tim to steal home. Jesse's eager too. He shifts from foot to foot, gripping and regripping the bat. He swings too fast for a little league pitch. He strikes out. The morning breeze rustles the new leaves on trees lining the field until they shimmer in colors of teal and gray-green. The mountains beyond envelop us in a canyon that echoes the cracking bats and cracking voices of young boys. I love it in the hills, but remain cognizant that this is a beautiful sport wherever it is played. Next inning: Tim is up. Bases loaded. Close game. He wallops it right back to the pitcher and his teammate is barely caught sliding home. The next hit, direct to second, takes Tim out, retiring the side.

Baseball is a game of failures, as school is for some. And it is a game for kids who are ever ready to get up, brush off, and try again, as school must become. Bases loaded again, and down by two, I snap to attention when Tim is up again. On the first pitch he pokes it past the shortstop for a RBI. Tie game. Baseball is a game of superstition, too. The state tournament started last week and the head coach for the high school team asked Jeff to assist him. The tournament weekend began with a traditional coaches' lunch at which they had to order Chinese food for luck. Jeff's fortune cookie was not encouraging about victory. "So I hid it," he confided with his wry smile.

Our new Emate laptop computer came in the mail Friday. It allowed me to spend the day writing out in the sun, or in front of TV, or in bed without having to retype everything later. I especially like that now I can specifically describe key moments in the boys' lives including on the ball field.

Well, this new freedom doesn't last long. Since Tim got home from school, the only time I get to use it is when he's asleep. That's great. He has typed a total of two pages in two days, more than he has ever typed in his life, and I'm sure his speed has doubled. Best of all, with no games on this laptop computer, the only activities available to Tim are typing and drawing. First he types out; "I love my new Emate." Then he asks me to dictate to him letter by letter so that he can practice his typing speed. I orally spelled out: "W-i-t-h this I can write as clearly and as well as anybody." Reading what he typed, he grins.

The Emate has changed the way that Tim approaches academics from the first. He loves the feeling of his fingers clicking the smooth, green keys and the fresh and neat new appearance of his written word. He seems to regard his favorite font, "casual," as the signature he never had. Most promising are the laptop's capabilities with an instant spell checker and a drawing program. He cannot wait to take it to school. There he uses it to take notes for his biography of Babe Ruth, and then his teacher, also intrigued by the Emate, teaches him to use it to make his notes into a perfect outline. I wonder what effect this tool will have on his success in middle school. It certainly helps us decide to go ahead and push him to go to Watkinson. At our public middle school, he wouldn't use a laptop; it would stigmatize him and might be stolen. Whereas, with its small classes and focus on individual learning styles, at Watkinson he won't be alone. We send in our deposit and put our house on the market to pay the balance, glad that the year away has softened the toughest barrier to getting any kid to change schools, leaving his friends.

Jeff and Matt's Plymouth Babe Ruth team struggle through the beginning of the summer season. As Jeff barks at them one night,

"I'm sorry if I'm hurting anybody's feelings, but it shouldn't surprise any of you to hear that we are not hitting, throwing, or fielding as well as we need to in this league." Since then he and another Jeff, the coaches, have been riding the boys hard, though not as hard as the other teams will ride them in competition. First, the coaches have the team practice the perfect throw, without a ball. The boys look, and feel silly, but no one has to catch or to follow the ball, so they focus on their form alone.

Next, Jeff asks me to videotape batting practice. Initially, the boys mug for the camera, but after a few of Jeff's shirt swiping inside heaters, they focus their attention and their swings. Drawn by human flesh standing stock still, mosquitoes and black flies abandon the woods surrounding the field to light on me. Thus, some of my camera work swoops and dives as I smack stingers on my knuckles, my ankles, and my throat. My biggest mugger, Johnny, who calls me mom, becomes my rescuer, fetching bug spray and chair to steady my hands. Matt, always my valiant protector, carries a net across the field to set up between any foul line drives and me. With such solicitation and a hug of thanks from Jeff after practice, I feel like a queen bee and a part of my boy's education again.

The team plays the next day, and boy they hit. Matt, who viewed the tape of his hitting and immediately recognized the mistake that his father has been telling him about for a week, finally gets his solid line drive back. Still, the team struggles on defense. As the sun drops and the trees extend long, gloomy fingers over the field, the boys allow walks and sustain errors until the bases are loaded. Part of their problem is chemistry. They haven't gelled as a team yet. At one low point, three players run up, stop, and stare at a bunted ball, waiting to see who will field it. Meantime the runner takes the base they have given him. When will they shake their early adolescence and take responsibility? I guess that's the greatest gift this game has to give to youth. At some point each kid has to step up to the plate and take charge of his own destiny.

With my Holderness students already on summer vacation and money running a bit short, I have signed up to substitute teach in the public schools. My first call requires me to teach in Matt's eighth grade wing of the middle school. I expect him to cringe. He does, but a sweet grin betrays that it's alright for me to accept the position. I'll just have to play it cool.

When we get to school, his pace quickens nervously, and I hang back so that he will not have to walk in with me: an adolescent nightmare. Without looking back, he waves a big hand over his red head appreciatively. I spend most of the morning out of sight, working in the computer room helping one of Matt's friends complete a long overdue essay. Before lunch, Matt has a class in the same room, and while his friends greet me excitedly with "Mrs. Ross, what are you doing here?" Matt deigns to give me only a quick nod late in the period. His house, his rules. I bow to his dignity.

At lunch I studiously ignore him, but as I eat my desert with my new colleagues, he stuns me by plopping down next to me and smiling. He knows. My surprise passes as he inevitably asks, "Do you have any money?" I don't. Undefeated, he willingly takes my ice cream to polish it off in front of his friends, figuratively rubbing their noses in his good fortune. He must have received a positive report from my student, because during his free period he elects to come to the computer room and to plop down right next to me. Though still busy with his buddy, I give him a discreet rub on the back and enjoy his presence thoroughly. How differently he would have responded a year ago. Is it his maturity, the time we have spent together this year, or the accepting nature of his friends up here in our beloved boondocks?

At the end of the day, my boys pile into the car with three friends, and we all drive to Concord to see the high school team battle for the state baseball championship. On the way we stop for Pringles, grapes, and Barqs root beer. The ride, a loud and riotous run from school, leaves the car a mess but the boys, utterly happy.

The game resembles a country fair. The other team strings helium balloons from the stands and the dugout. Half our town has driven an hour to be here, and no one looks disappointed. Expressing solidarity, the girls' softball team wears their uniforms and matching French braids with team-colored ribbons. Tim's friends toss popcorn at each other and pop each other's bright pink bubbles of gum creating cotton candy grins on their faces. Matt's crowd sits stock still next to the girls they have donned way too much cologne for. Nine bright bands of light guard the field against the darkening marine blue sky, which is interrupted only by a fat, luminous moon. Venus blinks at wisps of coral-colored clouds softly blanketing the sun as it sets for the night. Through sudden silence, the Star-Spangled Banner croons in tinny tones over the loudspeaker, and my heart pounds beneath my pledging hand in anticipation of the crack of the first bat. It's an idyllic night game in small-town America.

Ultimately, as deflated as their balloons, the opposing team wilts as our hometown crowd hoots and hollers our team to a narrow victory. Night brings a game-ending double play, which beacons the outfielders in doing handsprings on the pitcher's mound. Jeff beams as he claps each of his players on the back saying, "That's what it's all about!" After the award presentation, I congratulate Spencer, the coach's son who went to the Draper Camp with us in March, struggled while there to change his hitting, then batted .500 for the rest of the season. I give him a shiny penny I found at the concession stand just before the game. Superstitious, he accepts it reverently and, with a grateful grin, carefully places it in a case next to his award and looks deep into my eyes with a solemn nod that says that he will never play another game without it. I tousle his hair and move on through the crowd, truffled with celebratory cigar smoke. Reluctantly, we finally leave the field, savoring the moment and the company.

The celebration continues, however. One of the boys on the bus blares music to which Jeff boogies in the isle: the goofy side of their coach that the boys haven't seen before. When the bus turns off the highway at Plymouth, a waiting town police cruiser leads it on a loop through town, sirens wailing, followed by a caravan of fans in their cars honking and whistling. I suspect that almost everyone in every home we pass knows who we are and why we are making such a ruckus: small town spirit.

The right technology is a wonderful aid, especially to a child with a disability. Tim is already using his Emate at school to take notes, practice typing, create outlines, schedule assignments and organize his friends' phone numbers. The latter is a key to his independence, because it is so intrinsically motivating to this social guy and because the paper phone book has been such a tough hurdle for him, requiring flexible memory and reliable alphabetical sequencing skills. However, issues arise. We have not been able to transfer our writing on the Emate to the word processor on our home computer, so I spend a full morning reading all the information in the user's manual and running through each step of the two tours installed on the laptop. This critical function is not explained, so I call the Apple technological support line. After waiting thirty minutes to speak with a representative, a thoughtful gentleman walks me through each step including convincing my desktop computer that it has more memory than it really does. Yes, it is possible to lie to your computer! He and I have a good chuckle over this. Later, though, I still cannot transfer my writing from the Emate to my desktop computer, so I make a cup of tea and call again. Thank goodness I have time; what do most working parents do?

It takes even longer to get through the second time. The technological assistant, a short-tempered young man named Mike, spouts off a brief and highly technical answer to my question. "Wait," I cry, "you're going to have to walk me through this." He sighs, slows down, and speaks with unmistakable exasperation. As I struggle with a computer that will not react as he claims it will, I can hear him typing at a high speed. Clearly he is working on something else. Finally, when I hit a real dead end, he asks me to wait while he opens his computer to simulate the function I've been attempting. The other representative had worked with me attentively throughout the call! I am fuming.

Finally, he suggests that I buy ClarisWorks for my main computer, and I give him a terse, "I am sorry I took up so much of your time. Goodbye." I don't wait for his reply. I have enough information to figure that my Emate may be more compatible with Microsoft Word than with Microsoft Works. No problem; both are installed on my computer. After playing with the RTF and Text only settings, I figure out a cumbersome and rudimentary system for exporting my documents effectively from the Emate to the main computer. Suffering through one crash when my computer freezes, I have no alternative but to turn it off and pray that it will restart without doing any damage to the files. All survive, and I have a heck of a lesson to share with the kids tonight. I wonder what high point and low point of their days will be shared.

One weekend at the lake, the boys and their friend, Phil, enjoy all my favorite moments from growing up in Wolfeboro. Their antics give me a warm sense of continuity of shared childhood experience. First, they run straight to the tree house that Jeff and I built with Tim, and set up the zip line, a fifty-foot cable between two trees, for rides after dinner. They scold Brittany for irrepressibly diving into the waves as soon as we aren't looking. They paddle boats, shoot slingshots, spit watermelon seeds, build a fire, cook S'mores, unroll sleeping bags, and skinny dip – three pale moons dancing and diving beneath the original. Their voices ring out across the water, announcing their nakedness and their joy, while evoking my smile. Lying in my mother's room at the lake, considering a nap, I reread the poem Matt wrote sitting on the end of the dock one twilight, when he was just eight:

The Lake

The water gently lapping against the rocks.

The stars arranged in a bouquet of light.

The crickets chirping and the boats dancing

to a silent but beautiful song:

the song of the lake.

Matthew Brooks Ross

I turn my awareness to the hush of the waves on the shore beneath us as I listen to my mother's soft Bostonian accent reviewing the list of chores that we will attend to when we feel like getting up. Breathing deeply to savor the slight smell of pine needles and moth balls lingering in Dad's old Navy blankets, I feel deliciously tired from lugging the boats to the shore, hitting two doubles in a rousing game of wiffleball and hiking through the woods with Britty and Mum to get our official, annual count of lady slippers. Satisfied that at least twenty have survived, and thus that the woods remain stable, I allow myself to drift off to the sounds of the lake, the loons, and Mum's murmur. I drop taut shoulders and relax – sliding home.

I awake to the sounds of children returning from a late mini-golf game in Wolfeboro, eight miles away. We meet them in the kitchen where we share the first sweet, dripping blueberry pie of the season from the Yum Yum Shop Bakery. Mum whispers that she can tell that Tim was the low man. He doesn't look dejected, just lacks his usual bounce, and fails to give us an instant report on the game. Uncanny about Tim's moods, she's guessed right again.

Only twenty minutes later Tim finds two major distractions. "Snake!

Snake!" He cries as Phil runs for a flashlight and a bucket. While they dance around it, daring each other and asking me how to grasp it, I cautiously reach for its neck, suppressing my own trepidation, and hold it for them to stroke. Phil declines, backing up and wondering with his nose wrinkled, "How can you hold it?" Tim runs for a larger bucket, but before he returns, the snake panics, whips its surprisingly strong tail around my arm and oozes a skunky smelling musk, so I let it go. In the habit, especially this year, of looking up everything, we identify it as a ribbon garter snake, indigenous to New England, and as I expected, harmless. As Tim searches to find it again under a rock, Phil throws a fishing line out off the dock and instantly catches a good-sized smallmouth bass. With Tim's help he tries to play it in, letting it run, then reeling it in, but with one swift yank it breaks free, swimming away in a long dark shadow, promising to be our uncatchable, golden pond "Walter" of the season. We look it up on our pond life guide as well, enjoying natural learning moments that, with homeschooling behind us, Jeff and I need not push but still enjoy thoroughly.

Bob, my older brother, joins us for the weekend with his three children, so I get to pull godmother duty while he helps Mum put the mast in the sailboat and the motor on the put-put. In my own ancient playpen, bought with the lake cottage when I was one year old, same-aged Rebecca plays and gurgles with cups of lake water. Every so often she falls silent. Looking down from my writing, I am met by the epitome of the "Merry Twinkle," my mother's name for her latest grandchild. Her lake blue eyes meet mine solemn, then crinkle into eyelashes and light when I coo, "Becca-Becca-boo!"

As Anna Quindlin describes in her column "Mother of Sons," I too always, but only figuratively, kept an infant's dress in the bottom drawer of my dresser for the daughter I never had. My family has a Paul Revere teapot that has been handed down to eight generations of Susans and Sarahs. I never had my Sarah. But from our first meeting, Rebecca's big sister, Madeline, had been drawn to me and I to her. At family gatherings, she would slink shyly about until I would engage her in a discussion of, say, blankee fabric, making my lap available but resisting the urge to pull her to me. She did everything in her own time. So much more mature now, when she feels that baby Becky has monopolized my attention long enough, she wins my heart and my time with a hairbrush and a request for a French braid: my dream come true, to brush my little girl's hair. Having long ago had enough of her dark, damp locks falling long and chaotic over her face and shoulders, Bob responds with grateful eyes when I finish, and Madeline runs up the rocky bank of the lake to play wiffle ball with her brother Sam, her neat ponytail bouncing behind her. I love living so close to my young nieces and nephew and holding them close just as I begin to let my own boys go.

In the morning I awake to the rattle of a woodpecker that I had seen the day before, large and black with a fire-colored crest. I follow the solitary sound to our secluded, little beach and step in to rinse my feet. The cool, placid mirror barely stirs and entices me farther, as I hike up my white, cotton nighty and feel the baptismal water caress my knees, my legs, and my belly – soft and chubby from childbirth. My crusty eyes blink off sleep and reflect the reluctant mist hovering over the water, the stillness of the morning, and three, curious fish swarming and nibbling at my toes. A wood duck swims by with eight tiny babies on its back. Suddenly abandoned they paddle nervously in the water as she dives for food, then scramble back on board when she resurfaces to carry them off to another fishing site. Two sparrows swoop by as I rise and step out of the lake, letting my nightgown fall dripping around my ankles. Morning has broken.

The day progresses idyllically. Maddie asks to write imaginary letters on my back for the period of a full massage therapy treatment. Next, she asks to style my hair, another half-hour of relaxing pleasure. By mid-morning, I pack them up with Tim and Phil and take them all to town to buy honey-corn bread and gingerbread men at the Yum Yum Shop. We then race to lick drippy chocolate and black raspberry ice cream cones on the hot, town docks as the huge Mount Washington ship cruises into harbor and blasts its foghorn, announcing its arrival.

Our return to the cottage provides cool relief. My nieces' squeals greet me as I run along the bank, down the stairs, and off the dock in a shallow dive that takes me halfway to the raft that Dan built. Once there, I throw the two twelve-year-olds into the water and watch a sailboat that has turtled as its crew struggles to right it. Tim proudly explains to his friend that we stand ready to rescue them, that we've done it before, but the sailors soon manage admirably without need for our motor power. I envy them, and promise myself a sail with Mum when the wind calms. Meanwhile, savage white-capped waves ravage the naked, silver undersides of leaves along the shore, betraying a coming storm. I dive back into the water and swim deep below a line of yellow pollen that coats the surface at the edge of the trees' shadow line. The water chills me and each rock looms ominous before me. I skim by, regardless. Popping out next to my nephew, Sam, I catch him in a great, chilly hug then send him off to the "king of the raft" shoving match with the older boys. The lake has always been, will always be, the place where our family centers itself. For all my parents' progeny, the lake, if nothing else, is home.

I return to Windsor on my birthday. Early for an interview with Saint Joseph College's director of student teacher placements, I sit outside for a spell. I cannot help comparing Connecticut to my birth state, wondering if I should come back here at all. Listening, I hear that the birds sing just as eagerly, though they are higher pitched warblers. Gazing, I find the sky just as blue, though airplanes occasionally split it with a white line and white noise; and the sun shines as brightly, really more so, which I love in May and hate in July. I duck in to meet with the director, who I like and trust immediately, and I find myself hired on the spot to supervise student teachers and to guide them to improve their teaching skills. That's it then. We are coming back. Little did I expect such opportunities to materialize so soon. Eager to reach more students' lives, to defend their rights to an appropriate education by training their teachers, I am suddenly, deliciously, excited to return to Connecticut in spite of my love for those New Hampshire hills. Windsor gardens pop with blooms of pink, lavender, and maroon irises, beckoning me home.

I celebrate on my way back to New Hampshire by stopping at Yankee Candle which offers an impressive collection of shops, with a room filled with candles for every state, a room filled with Christmas ornaments, and a room where the boys would love making their own candles: another field trip perhaps. A mixture of lovely, simple gardens, soft jazz playing "Our Love is Here to Stay," and a multitude of scented candles make it an inviting retreat. I recall dancing to the song on one of our anniversaries, and I am eager to celebrate my birthday and Father's Day with Jeff. I begin to believe in aromatherapy and look forward to filling my home with the soothing scent. I select a sweet, crisp Honeydew in a soft sage green. A large candle for me and dining room candles for Jeff.

Late in the day, my return home is melancholy. An empty house greets me. and I notice that my tires are getting bald, an expense we don't need. I look at the fridge where Jeff's note reads:

Suz,

I'm at D&M field umpiring a little league play off game(?!) Matt is scheduled to get in about 6:30 (Someone called to tell us). If Tim isn't home, he is at D&M on his bike.

See ya, Jeff

So I pour myself a bowl of my guilty favorite, Frosted Flakes, for my birthday dinner, but find that the milk supply has not been replenished. Powdered milk does not taste as good on my cereal as it had on my hiking trip last August. After washing my dishes, I drive down to the school to collect Matt. As I am looking across the field for him, he sneaks up from behind and gives me a rough hug around the shoulders. I chuckle, pleased to find him so demonstrative at school.

We buzz down to join Jeff for the game, and we all go out for ice cream afterward, not for my birthday, but because a friend of Tim's is going, and Jeff wants to talk with his father about baseball. Again, baseball seems to come before family, or we are just ships passing in the night. I am peeved.

In the evening, Jeff slumps in front of a baseball game on TV, understandably exhausted from coaching and having the kids to himself, and then sits stock-still and silent when the boys flatly refuse plans we have made for Tim to be tutored in phonics this summer and for Matt to attend confirmation classes in the fall. I know that he assumes that his silence is supportive, that their defiance will pass if ignored, but I think the boys read his silence as indifference. Later, as I settle into bed to read, Jeff comes upstairs early. But, again, he makes no mention of my birthday or the boys' behavior. He wants to discuss summer baseball options for Tim. I go to bed feeling cranky, old, and alone, but mostly concerned that the boys need us to teach them so much more than academics. They need us to show them that marriage is a united effort, to support one another and to celebrate one another. A birthday offers an apt opportunity and a good moment for the boys to learn to appreciate us, but no one reminded them of this on this forgotten birthday. I pout.

In the morning, in a more proactive mood, I suggest that four new radials would make a great birthday present. Initially, Jeff seems happy to get off the hook so practically, but later that morning, he surprises me with a true celebration by taking me shopping for a dress I've coveted for weeks and hiking boots I'm going to need on the Appalachian Trail with Cath in August. Then we walk down to a friend's sister's new restaurant, Main Street Station. It replaced a shabby, old diner that inhabited an old railroad car. Maryjo joins us for a birthday hug and a drink. She plans to evaluate Tim to document his academic progress this year. I can't wait to see how his reading scores have changed. His newfound success and confidence in school reassures me, but test scores will provide the more objective indicator that Watkinson needs to determine his abilities and his curriculum.

Matt's graduation from Plymouth Elementary School is an authentic, loving tribute, with silhouettes of each eighth grader adorning the stage. The only decorations necessary, they focus our attention appropriately on the kids, seated on stage in two rows. The brilliance of the ceremony shines in its simplicity and in holding the students together, directing their attention to one another, and helping them to value each other's unique spirit. I once read that a great hostess brings her guests not to her but to each other. The boys' principal has mastered this approach. I vow to do the same for my students and for my boys, encouraging them to depend on each other, not on me. Jacqueline Kennedy once told a reporter that her best life's work was in raising her children to be each other's closest friends, an admirable goal.

Everybody can be great…because anybody can serve. You don't have to have a college degree to serve. You don't have to make your subject and verb agree to serve. You only need a heart full of grace. A soul generated by love.

- Martin Luther King, Jr.

The eighth graders sit facing each other and giggling most of the time. There's plenty to chuckle at. Several boys have new buzz cuts and some girls have opted for their first formal up sweeps. Otherwise it's an informal moment. The principal teases his students, most for more than eight years, Matt of only two months, yet fully included in the fun. A chronic gum chewer receives a plaque with a wad of wet gum on it. Melinda, a darling space case, accepts the astronomy award, giggling; the school does not offer astronomy. One mother reads a poem in which she speaks my heart saying, "I love you like I breathe, I can't control it." I glance at Matt: handsome in his designer vest and the shirt I bought for Jeff's birthday. Jeff spent the afternoon washing and ironing it while I delivered soda and pizza for the graduation dance tonight. I beam as the principal gives Matt an award for his invention of a tear-away baseball warm up, and a coach's award from his baseball coach and algebra teacher, Spence. Grateful, we hug Spence later, and he reminds us of yet another teaching position we should consider. He loves coaching with Jeff and has gotten into an endearing habit of egging us on to stay in Plymouth. We lean toward the temptation, having just sniffled through a slide show full of our town's children's grins from kindergarten through last week's eighth grade trip to Montreal. The strains of the last song playing "hold a place in your hearts for when we return" hold special meaning for us and for our friends in Plymouth. We plan to return to Connecticut in August, but we hope to return to Plymouth in another era, perhaps when Tim hits high school, perhaps when we retire. It has become home.

The next morning, as the soft, silent sun peeks out over the Holderness hills, I peek in at our sleeping children as I used to when they were small. Their relaxed cheeks and soft mouths look so much the same. I inhale, long and deep, as love rushes through me, inebriating.

My Boys of
Summer

To his dismay, Jeff and I signed Tim up for summer tutoring with Mrs. Howe, a phonics teacher trained in Orton-Gillingham and Lindamood-Bell approaches. I hold my breath, hoping it will work out. I believe in the whole language approach to reading, but too many of Tim's teachers have embraced the free reading, invented spelling and sight word approaches while neglecting the comparative drudgery of teaching phonics: big mistake. Whole language was never intended to neglect phonemic awareness training. Children need phonetic training integrated into a stimulating, whole language curriculum:

hence the word "whole!" Tim and so many of his peers with learning disabilities throughout the country do not catch on to the code of the English language as naturally as most do. Now that he is old enough to appreciate its importance, I want to see to it that Tim learns to decode words once and for all. Remediation is best achieved in the elementary years, which are rushing to an end for Tim. After that time, mistakes are more ingrained, difficult to unlearn and teaching compensation is often found more efficient than remediating deficiencies.

Surprising him on our arrival, Mrs. Howe asks Tim what he feels he needs work on this summer, offers him an unlimited supply of Twizzlers, and plays cards with him – a phonics card game. They hit it off. I exhale. During the game she pinpoints some of the suffixes with which he is not familiar. On one occasion she catches my eye as he reads "puddle" for "bubble." Visually and auditorily, he confuses ps, bs, and ds. Visually, he reverses or transposes them; auditorily, he fails to catch their brief beginning sounds, the only distinguishing cue. Later she coaches him to use colored blocks to signify changing blended sounds. She corrects him gently. "No, stop. I want you to think in terms of sounds not letters." Even now, his previous years of silently completing worksheets at school have taught him to look not to hear. Soon he recognizes how to change the sound "ent" to "eng," and replaces the appropriate letter block. Einstein's light bulb flashes. "Oh!" he exclaims. "That makes it easier." She gets him to supplement his weak auditory awareness with his strong kinesthetic awareness by making him aware of the location and feeling of his tongue and lips as he makes each sound. This he can do. Her version of the Lindamood Bell LIPS approach to phonemic awareness works for Tim. On our way out she cheers, "See you tomorrow, Tim!" He groans, but he does not balk.

Afterward we follow her directions just a mile up the road to Mirror Lake where Tim enjoys his first dalliance of the summer in his precious, yellow kayak. The one he earned last fall. The pond is clear and closely surrounded by pine-studded hills on all sides. No wind disturbs the mirror. Gray boulders, white birch trees, and one cheerful, yellow house punctuate the shore. After gently paddling to the far shore and exploring an inlet, Tim glides back to me and the beach, where he gives me an impish glance and flips the kayak, drenching himself and startling me. For a moment I see nothing but yellow plastic and ripples, then he pops up to the surface grinning like the sun.

The next day I want to soften the trip to Mrs. Howe's again with another activity that Tim will find inherently enjoyable. So we leave early and stop at Holderness School on our way to the lesson. The school's art teacher meets us as planned, and we throw clay on pottery wheels for an hour. Tim has a real flair for ceramics, and it tests his patience without exasperating him. His first attempt becomes too muddy and flops. It relieves him to take the sloppy mess over to the cement table and slam it around until the clay and his temper become more composed. Then he creates a pretty graceful candleholder. I feel closer to discovering his talents and his path. Planning to return in the afternoon to attach a handle, Tim grows excited to give it to his dad for a belated birthday gift to go with the candles I gave him on Father's Day. I fashion a candle holder as well. The clay spins between my fingers, soft and wet. Centering it is frustrating, but once done, the self-supporting form responds to every pressure symmetrically. I like symmetry; it's comforting and predictable. I no longer feel like the strained potter, vigorously trying to raise and to center this family. I feel a part of an amorphous form that continuously rights and loses and rights itself again: family-centered.

Again, at the lake days later, my lungs and my soul fill with the luscious scents of cedar shingles, smoldering coals and pine needles from outside the screened-in porch and from thirty-eight summers before. I love having this refuge from my childhood so close by. This is our homestead, the place we all call home. Last night, as has been our habit for years, Jeff and I pored over real estate ads, anticipating the day when we can provide such a homestead near here for our children's children. Sitting in the rocker mom and I recovered with orange fabric in the seventies, I breathe deeply and feel the forest air oxygenating my body, tingling my fingers and toes. The lake, softly lit in layers of gray mist, barely gives way as a canoe passes by, its paddles sweeping the air and dripping gently on the still water. A solitary loon bobs in the distance, occasionally crooning then falling silent. The gentle white noise of night and the lapping of the waves on the shore dissipate. The world stands still, dozing as it listens for daybreak: the melding of the last hoots of the barn owl and the piercing "You who!" of the mourning dove, the rustle of early breezes and the yellow light of leaves refracting the rising sun. I doze too.

By the time my boys lumber down the stairs from their dark, pine-shaded bedrooms the dock is fully sunlit. They are surprised it is past mid-morning. They gobble up honey-corn toast and dicker over whether to play Monopoly or Wiffle Ball first. Matt wins; no surprise. Listening to them hit fouls to the old tree swing, base hits past the retired sailboat, and outs against the trees. I realize that they haven't complained about going to the cottage, about its lack of television or video games at all this summer. They had in the past, but now they create their own entertainment, while I make home. The paper and coffee wait for Jeff as steak marinades and red potatoes boil. I mince onions, peppers, and parsley for three kinds of potato salad – my new forte. I set the table for lunch with Mum's bright, ancient Fiestaware. She always scoffs when people mention it. "I got it at the grocery store when you were kids!" I put my favorite navy blue plate at my place with the view of the lake, knowing that Tim or Matt will switch it unless theirs are green. I set old grape jelly jar glasses for them, one printed with the Flintstones and one with the presidents through Kennedy, dating when we got it precisely. I scrub petrified chocolate and marshmallow off of the new, alien looking microwave that defies the antiquity of our cottage. The boys used it to make S'mores last night when it was too hot for a fire. Rubbery and uncharred, the marshmallows hardly qualified for wanting s'more. Neglecting the dishes, we had elected instead to rinse the stickiness off our bodies in the dark, lukewarm lake before slipping under cotton sheets to sleep with sinful ease in the midst of New England's first heat wave of the summer. I love being far from the smoggy suburbs in this weather.

A coup. After coffee and the paper, Jeff distracts the boys with a game of Sorry long enough for me to swim out for the boat, collect the life preservers and call the family down to the dock for a motorboat ride around the lake. It's about time for the boys to learn how to handle the boat on their own. They each have a lesson, filling them with surges of power and glee. Matt is characteristically cautious and responsible at first, then guns it toward Stamp Act Island. Tim watches with twitchy impatience for his turn. At that point he plops down next to me and guns it right away. He soon loses control of the handle. We spin in tightening circles over mounting, crisscrossing wakes. Tim and Matt freeze, wide eyed, looking at me. Jeff catches my eye and grins. As he would have it, I let it continue to turn erratically – long enough for a little fear to teach the boys. Then I right the motor, and we ask them what could have happened. Discussion ensues; then lesson learned, we continue on. Taking turns, neither Matt nor Tim lets go again. Soon we speed across the lake and past Governor's Rock where we tell them how Mrs. John Wentworth, wife of the last royal governor of New Hampshire, didn't like life in the boonies according to our treasured, old book, *The Governor's Lady*, by Thomas H. Raddall. So, she had her staff, probably slaves, take her out to the rock for a parasol picnic each day.

We motor on to see an isolated turn-of-the-century cottage with a long porch to the water. Always dreaming of living here forever, it is Jeff's favorite – a yellow Victorian with a mysterious, long house next to it, barely visible through the trees. We peer in and speculate that it might be a bowling alley or a rifle range. Jeff explains that it could have been slave quarters in Victorian days, or we prefer to think, it may have been built to accommodate run-away slaves on the Underground Railroad. We think it's a great hideout and are proud of Wolfeboro and Windsor's abolitionist history. Turning home, we pass our third and fourth loons of the day. Encouraging. I remind the kids of how the Lake Wentworth Association has worked to protect the loon population, just as it worked, years ago, to purchase the expansive Stamp Act Island out of the hands of condominium developers. It's now completely undeveloped and the home of the largest blue heron colony in New England. Score one for a childhood preserved. Later, on the road home to Plymouth, we pass an old Burma Shave ad in the form of a series of signs saying, "In this land / of toil and sin, / your head grows bald / but not your chin." This land filled with "Tuck Me Inns," "Ta da Dump" roads and "Curl Up & Dye" hair salons, has a corny simplicity that catches us giggling, unabashed. It sweetens the soul.

A family's soul is recorded in shared memories, and today we set off to make a memory. Having won a day trip to Cow Island on Lake Winnipesaukee in a silent auction at Holderness School, we maneuver the boys away from TV and friends and onto a boat tied to the pier at Meredith. Tim checks out each nook of the ample sleeper with two beds, a kitchenette, and a head. During the twenty-minute ride to the island, Matt tries to maintain a frown, having been taken from his friends, and we sightsee Mounts Major, Gunstock, Rattlesnake and even Chocorua. We make a pact that we will climb Red Hill later this summer to see Lake Winnipesaukee and both Squam Lakes at our feet. On the way across the big lake, we stop to hike the new preserve, Ragged Island, before continuing on to Cow Island, where, our host tells us, the first Guernseys from Scotland were quarantined in the nineteenth century only to become the most common cow in America today. Our hosts offer a fascinating tour and another educational field trip for us all. Even Matt gives way to his curiosity and begins to ask questions about the expansive lake.

After a picnic of KFC and hot dogs cooked on sticks over a fire, we walk to the beach on the other side of the island and swim with a mink whose droppings mark our trail back to the boat. Once there, we climb aboard, motor out to the Broads, the deepest, widest part of the lake, then cut the engine, giving way to the highlight of the trip. Matt and Tim laugh and whoop as our host leads them in a swim, plunging off the roof of the boat into deep waters. I can't resist for long. My head hits the water hard, like a mallet breaking glass, and then all I feel is cool relief and silky water everywhere. I work my way to the surface, a canopy of blue, and to the shouts of my boys, "Watch this, Mom!" Tim, in particular, cannot enjoy an experience quite so much if I don't witness it. I concede; that won't last forever.

We join our neighbors, Marie and Jerry, for the community's celebration of the Fourth of July. Small town pride feeds patriotism. After doling out five-dollar bills and sending six boys off to the midway, the two couples celebrate our independence. We watch our neighbors and gossip and plan baseball strategies, until the boys return with tiny, plastic army men that they won throwing darts at balloons and with fried dough disgustingly drenched with maple syrup, powdered sugar, and cinnamon. The fireworks start slowly after firemen pass the hat for next year's display. I warn Matt not to expect the show we've become accustomed to in the city where it is budgeted into a large, annual civic budget. Boy am I mistaken. The show bubbles and bursts into a rolling boil of explosions and light in whites, greens, reds, and blues. My favorite – the white works that sizzle into many whirling stars that whistle through the sky – lead into the grand finale. The only thing missing is the sound of the symphony playing Tchaikovsky's Eighteen-Twelve Overture. Passing by scads of our neighbors dressed in red, white, and blue or veteran's uniforms and waving small flags or tired toddlers, we revel in a collective pride in our country, in our freedom, and in our mountains' majesty. As we inch home, even the traffic resembles that in Hartford. Happy and enervated, we wonder again, why leave this community we love so much next month?

With school out, my boys settle into a contented routine of baseball and mountain life, I take a new plunge toward my development as a writer and attend the UNH writing project for three weeks. At our first meeting, writer Donald Murray speaks brilliantly in his voice of the common man. He interrupts reading his work often to share with us what he was thinking and how he mulled over what he wrote, reconsidering each phrase for wording and pace. He defines the voice of a writer and charges us to develop our own. So, we write. I write.

We write, then slink away for a quick bite and wine, which leads to a sunset sharing of our stories for suggestions and support. Stories of fathers' gentle hands, now available only through prayer, of mothers' roles reversed in the face of cancer, of babies long-desired and miscarried in a pool of blood and regret, and of eye-clouding depressions eased by a hairdresser who lifted one's hair so tenderly that for a moment he became the lover of one's dreams. At an unassuming Durham café, what Mar Pearl refers to as the "felt sense" of the writer rises from each of us in turn like the rich notes of an oboe rising above a gentle nest of clarinets. This sharing, collective writing really, leads me to tell tales I never knew I had to tell, first in our safe circle, then on the page; and in so telling, I learn more of why this family-centered year has been so important, why this book could be so important. My friends lean in to hear me as I lean in to hear them; this sharing leads us all late into the night. Late enough that I prefer to stay in the dorm and wash my face with paper towels rather than separate and go home. Or maybe I just don't want to leave the nest I have helped to create, weaving each solitary sentence together so intriguingly that the bond cannot be broken.

As highly skilled writers – though not trained in the gentle art of literary pointing – on weekends my family can provide an intimidating place to risk my writing, particularly because so much of it is about them. They want to fix it. They want to protect me from disappointment. Weekdays at UNH provide a parallel life. Writing is a dual life. I find I'm talking to myself with a purpose now, especially in the car – where no one lurks to question my sanity. I'm going to have to get a little tape recorder. It's dangerous to jot down ideas and descriptions when I'm driving and I am driving a lot, to and from home.

I meet my classmate, Samantha for breakfast and for a little conferencing. I am going to have to find someone in Connecticut who is as good at listening to my work, pointing out what works and sharing ideas for what deserves improvement – someone who just likes the sound of my words. I am going to have to become that someone for my students, focusing on their power first before acknowledging the flaws in their self-expression and strategizing ways to remediate. I find the power of such a relationship remarkable. I feel a calling. I used to think that I would never want to be a writer: too lonely. But now I feel I am never alone, because my reader is always with me, and my readers at UNH have been so empowering. In my gratitude, and in my love of working one on one with students, I want to pass the gift along.

Writing and Being by G. Lynn Nelson is a gorgeous book. Are we now, collectively, "taking back our lives through the power of language?" I find Native American lore touching and grounding. The idea of building a writing hogan, or creating a special corner of my home just for writing and listening appeals, a niche just for me. "May our time here together be quiet and attentive"(G.L. Nelson). Yet, my writing hogan seems to be a ballfield this summer, a sacred space in itself.

On the way to the semi-finals of the Babe Ruth district tournament, Matt wants to ride up in a coach's car with all of his friends. Who can blame him? But it's my last day with him before returning to the writing project, so I implore all of the kids to run up in my car. They express reluctance, afraid that I won't allow them to play their favorite tape. It blasts some revolting rap, but I willingly tune out illicit expletives and raunchy rhetoric in trade for two extra, precious hours with my boy. I have missed him while away for my graduate program, and, I admit, it stings a bit that he's been too busy to really miss me. So, to the displaced sound of blasting vulgarities, we drive through the pine-studded Franconia Notch, as Freckles, Johnny's three-week-old beagle puppy, sleeps behind me in his master's sun-tanned arms.

As we pass the chiseled chin of the Old Man in the Mountain, I ask the players to tell me when I should glance up, having seen it only once. Its chiseled features come to life at a critical moment as we drive by, and then recede into a typical Appalachian cliff, begging to be scaled. Fortunately, the eyes of one of the boys remain fixed on the mountain where he glimpses a brown mound waddling up one of Cannon's abandoned ski trails.

"Hey! Check out the bear!" All eyes search the hill and soon catch sight of the mobile mound and a speck of a cub following behind like the mama and cub in Robert McCloskey's *Blueberries for Sal.* One boy challenges the widely held theory that these are black bears, suggesting, "They're probably just raccoons."

"Oh, yeah, like we'd be able to see a raccoon from a mile away," another scoffs. The argument is sound – the debate, over.

Their ballgame ends as decisively and as victoriously as the bear debate. Even though, or perhaps because the opposing team arrives bemoaning the fact that they have to play Jeff and Matt's team even after beating them handily in the mid-season game. Their boasting enrages our boys, or they just finally come together as a team, because they trounce their opponents handily by the ten-run rule, mercifully ending the game in the sixth inning. I am still searching for the right words to describe the sound of young ball players' chatter. It's a monotone, like the rhythmic blast of the foghorn off Nubble Light, each voice tuned to the same G minor chord. It's a paradox, an enthusiastic lull. And this one lulls like slowly heating soup, preparing to boil over. I sit, an observer in my son's life, more than ever. Having been away at school all week and writing madly when I am home, I have lost my standing at the core of his life. He has grown accustomed to turning to Jeff and focusing on his friends, as well he should. Funny, a year ago I expressed such anxiety when he and Jeff left for a few weeks and they, we, were fine. Now, I have left for a few weeks and they, I, am fine. Even Tim, off skateboarding with Spence, seems happy and settled and is still working regularly with Mrs. Howe. And Jeff, missing me but strong and supportive, stands proud as the core, juggling all the boys' needs while I pursue a dream.

What a class. Something about Professor Carpenter's heart-on-his-sleeve teaching style and the way that he invites us to bring in personal artifacts and develop writing portfolios bonds this classful of independent writers quickly and irrevocably. He is aided by May, who gives us the story of "the little man," a toy she shared with her father for years before he died, hiding it in her newborn baby's hands and later finding it in her birthday cake. And he is abetted by Kelly, who writes of driving her mother to seventy-two body and soul wracking chemotherapy sessions, where a nurse with no warmth and no aim stabbed repeatedly at a vein and at our hearts. Their candid expressions press me to tell more, and what I tell, they want to hear. The lingering support of my classmates will help me make my daunting transition back to Connecticut and to my new hodgepodge of teaching opportunities which I hope will grow into a sound business of supporting students with special needs and encouraging them to share their stories, too.

Tomorrow I will attempt to create the ideal writer's workshop by taking the class to my cottage on Lake Wentworth and surrounding them with woods, rocks and other God-given writing hogans. My thanks to my classmates for when "two roads diverged in the wood," [they all promise to take] "the one less traveled by" in spite of the insistent call of deadlines, family, and work. Robert Frost would be pleased. They respond with instant enthusiasm, offering to bring hot dogs, bathing suits, pencils, and paper: all we will need. The weather supports our flight as well, rendering our U.N.H. classroom too sticky and stuffy for work and promising to be even hotter tomorrow. We'll be swimming.

While at Mom and Dad's in Exeter, I prepare for the retreat. As I collect paper goods left over from his wedding, my brother Dan comes by to wash his car. It seems like a good idea, and he already has all the gear out, so I wash mine too. I say little, he less. But we enjoy a connection, side by side, completing symmetrical turns of the hose. It is a pleasant deja vu to a thousand chores we shared in childhood, to a thousand water fights we don't need to repeat. It reminds me, again, of Anne Morrow Lindbergh's cherished *Gift of the Sea*, in which the Argonaut reminds her of the simple, silent joy of doing the dishes with her sister at her home by the shore. Brother, mine.

I drive up to the lake at night, and wouldn't you know? I awake to rain…and wouldn't you know? This hardy group still wants to come. So I sit now, enjoying the sound of the fire crackling, belated drops of rain falling hollowly on the roof, and Sheila, Christine and Liz exploding into laughter at Heidi's commentary on her writing portfolio – "isn't that prom dress the scariest thing you've ever seen?" Hot dogs eaten and paper plates burned, we pick at grapes and strawberries and fall to writing. I needlessly apologize for the soft sound of the keys on my laptop, breaking the still air in sync with the repetitive pop of pinesap torched and the occasional rip of pages removed, but not discarded. Suddenly we value our own every word, as we did while taking notes on Shelly Harwaynes' lecture describing her alternative middle school. We all want to find a school like hers, where a child would say that she wished school were over at twelve, meaning midnight. How will we make our classes feel like that in September? How will we carry the feeling of this unexpected classroom in the woods into our noisy, linoleum worlds? There is a hum in the room, our thoughts and souls pouring out into the air, our voices silently dropping on blank paper, coloring it with unique rhythms we hanker to share. I will miss this camaraderie, this parallel play at writing. But I can't wait to share this passion for learning what we each have to say with kids, especially my own. Guilt eases with the realization that by my very absence, I have expressed faith in them and set an example for lifetime learning, for pursuing a dream, for using writing as a life skill.

AUGUST

My last few weeks in Plymouth wash away with the boys, baseball, packing, and moving, and now I part from my family again for a few days' adventure. They busily settle into our home in Connecticut, utterly embraced by our old neighborhood, by fellow "faculty brats," Kelly, John, Robbie, and Russ, more siblings than friends to the boys. Meanwhile, as part of my renewed commitment to my family of origin, I help Cath, more family than friend to me – born four days before me when we were both faculty brats at Exeter – lead fifteen of her freshman across thirty miles of the Appalachian trail. Trudging along on a horrendous hike through pelting cold rain, we don't find the engaging energy we enjoyed last summer. The trail provides a rough haul, with many exhausting inclines, lots of tumbling terrain, and plenty of threatening poison ivy. The kids press on stoically, quiet and determined to make it to our campsite. One girl's ankle, sprained on a slippery slope, holds up, though she winces and leans heavily on me as we traverse the rocks. Breaks are necessarily brief and most of us remain standing on sore feet to avoid the wet and poison-ivied ground. I slip and strain my back while carrying our tent: an extra ten pounds on top of my pack, shaved to a mere twenty pounds itself. When we finally reach camp, Cath and I simultaneously grumble that we would rather give birth, and then smile wearily at our classic synchronicity. However, when we arrive at our campground on Annapolis Rocks, there is no time to recuperate. We first must erect six tents and a tarp to cook beneath. Then we chill for a brief rest.

Dangerous exhaustion sets in. We cannot imagine lifting our bodies again, but I must. Cath shivers with blue lips, and due to her diabetes, has few ways to warm herself. She already used up her energy on the hike and cannot run around like the kids to stay warm without plunging her blood sugar level dangerously low. I struggle to get some twigs burning, blowing at, and huddling by a spark of a fire. Finally, our Outward Bound-trained leader arrives and boots us into action again. He yanks off Cath's outer clothes and gives her his polypropylene pants and hat for warmth. When he turns his attention to me, I wave him off. Under a two-dollar pocket poncho, impulsively thrown into my pack, I have stayed remarkably dry, and subsequently warm enough. So, I join him in wrapping yesterday's sweaty shirts around cold student's heads to hold in warmth while leading them down to the spring, skipping and jump-jacking along the way to stave off hypothermia. Soon spring water boils on Cath's roaring fire and twenty of us huddle under the tarp and the split splat of the rain for cocoa and shared bodily warmth. I think of Jeff and our boys, how I would love to share such adventures with them, and more so, how I would love to be home, safe, and warm with them.

We wake from hard sleep to the remains of last nights' rain drizzling off the trees and patting on our tent and then splashing into our Earl Grey tea, then to blue sky and – eureka! - the sun. Finally, it breaks over our heads as clouds wisp by on the breeze lifting the mist that once occluded every sight but the closest cliffs that resembled eerie castle ruins in the rainy evening light. Now, for the highlight of our adventure, the reason for trudging all the way here. One of the girls scales a rock face thirty feet high, against a panoramic view of the Appalachian valley and the occasional, far off sounds of a road to civilization. Climbing with sure feet and grabbing with calloused fingers, she searches the small crevices and ridges where centuries of rainfall have washed away the softer limestone and sand from the granite cliff offering handholds and hope. Then, trying to circumvent a protruding branch, suddenly she goes flying, and I tighten my hold on her bole losing my footing as her weight yanks me up by the hips. Finally, I ground myself and she grasps a handhold, starting again for the top where she ultimately shouts and ecstatically kisses the carabineer.

Later, I am dubbed the fire goddess when we collect around a damp fire that no one believed could be lit. I learned a lot from that woodstove last winter. Restored by mesmerizing firelight, we celebrate the day as crickets whir – answering each other so loudly and repetitively that they sound orchestral – like my father sawing wood slowly, deliberately, melodiously, to make the cottage warm for his family. Our fire warms us too, as we sit in a Quaker silence, listening for signs of God. The Friends' School, students respond. With joyful tears they speak of the power of their teachers, of overcoming life-diminishing fears, of never knowing they could be so intensely bound to each other. That happened within the first hour on the trail. This group clicked and jelled, supporting each other in hardship; nourishing each other with song, humor and hugs; and motivating each other to new heights – literally, and figuratively. They pray their appreciation, confessing to new-school fears, fears no one has admitted before, confessing to lies, even those white ones they've told to keep themselves and each other safe, but apart. They won't let anything keep them apart anymore. The fire wanes, and we pass pressed hands, then meander with tent-fellows back to our soft shelters remembering relentless rains, fire goddesses, ghost stories, hot tea, and soft eyes glowing in the firelight, crinkled with smiles and acceptance and wandering to the stars.

The sun, still miraculous after the rains, blinks on the surface of the Shenandoah, our next challenge. Cath and I wake with our new tent mate, Niall, the river god, a dear young man from England who at Cath's command, "Niall, avert your eyes," dives into his sleeping bag in mock terror screaming, "I'm averting, I'm averting!" Dressed and up, Cath and I soon find private places in the woods for relieving ourselves and brushing our teeth. Morning rituals exclude our precious tea – no fuel left – we'll have to savor Earl Grey all the more when we get home tonight. Right now, I savor my sister soul's company as we anticipate our last day when we finally, somewhat selfishly, will let the students paddle ahead, in order to develop their independence and to let us linger together.

On the river, a riotous outcome punishes us for such self-indulgence. Two students zigzag for miles despite our careful and repeated instructions. Finally caught up on a ledge, they lose a paddle. Bad move. They drift around a small island, disembark, and hike across the landform expecting to find the paddle where they lost it – ignoring the obvious current. Observing them from a quarter mile downstream, we take the opportunity for a pit stop, thus forevermore referring to our predicament and their follies as "The Yellow Rock Incident." Waiting impatiently, we debate experiential education versus scaffolded instruction. Cath definitely wants to let them muddle through alone at whatever cost, while I yearn to provide them with reasonable opportunities for success despite their flailing twenty minutes behind the group, having only one paddle and lacking even a modicum of sense or ability. Inanely still paddling from the bow in spite of all our instructions to steer from the rear, they finally drift in, and I end our discussion of teaching styles by leaping into their boat. Even then, one student gets out on the downstream side, inviting disaster as the strong current bashes the canoe into him, knocking him off the slippery ledge and stealing away his sandal. The awkward adolescents' comedy of errors continues as Cath and I paddle from parallel sterns, unable to notice any difference as the students trade off using their one paddle to help. One of them chirps, "Wow! We are going so much faster now." To which the other concurs, "Yea! There must be something wrong with our boat!" Rolling our eyes, Cath and I look forward to retreating to dry land and to sharing the Yellow Rock story with Niall, on our way to see the Monkees' reunion tour in D.C. tonight.

Safely back in Washington, we find the Monkees' performance is equally riotous, as is the performance of their groupies throwing flowers and, astoundingly, underwear, onto the stage. When caught in the crowd and pressed to the front, Cath begins to feel shaky, having had no insulin for hours. Distressed to know that she is low again so soon after the hike, I beg an accommodating woman next to me for Starbursts, just the ticket. Soon after, drummer and ex-blues singer Mickey Dolenz steps forward to croon an old favorite blues tune, surprisingly well. During the saxophone solo, Niall dares me to hop up on stage and dance with Mickey. "Oh, no!" Cath gaffed, "Don't ever dare, Suz!" Sure enough, I impulsively push off from Niall's shoulder, hop up onto the stage, hold my arms out in a shrug and ask, " Mickey, would you like to dance?" Six bouncers rush the stage from either side, but Mickey waves them off authoritatively, takes me in his arms stiffly and waltzes me gracefully in a few tight circles, spinning me out every now and then. Finally, he spins me out into the outstretched hand of a smiling assistant, who leads me off the stage like a queen. On the way down the stairs, a huge, bald bouncer confronts us furiously and spits "Get! Her! Out!" The assistant leads me into the crowd and discretely turns me loose to return to Cath's and Niall's laughter and accolades. Out on the street after the show, a woman whispers excitedly behind us, "That's her!

That's the one who danced with Mickey!" And so, my fifteen minutes of fame and my remarkable retreat with the wondrous woman I grew up with concludes, and I head home at last, eager to share my adventures with my family and to make our old home our new world.

Fall Reflections:
Schooling Our Kids in Public,
at Home, and in Private

Back home in Connecticut and meeting with Matt's academic dean to plan his ninth-grade program, Jeff and I receive a call from our dear neighbor, Joanne, telling us to come home right away. Matt's been cut. Too frantic to retrieve the car with Jeff, I sprint across campus and arrive just before the ambulance. I find a pane of glass on our front door shattered in a web of sharp shards, blood splattered high on the walls and ceiling and floor, Brittany who has been carefully locked upstairs to keep her safe from the glass strewn on the floor, and the boys nowhere to be seen. Breathless, I finally find them next door. Matt, in good color, lies on his back with his lacerated wrist in the air where Joanne's husband, Norm, holds it hard, though it persists in bleeding through the once white tee-shirt Matt grabbed when he realized the danger he was in. He had cut his wrist deeply accidentally pushing his hand through our windowed door just as Tim closed it. In spite of quick action and cool heads, the EMT's estimate that he has lost almost a pint of blood. I fear he may have lost his dream to be a great catcher as well.

Twelve hours, an ambulance ride and two hours of microscopic surgery later, Matt wakes up in the postoperative room. Upon seeing me his eyes grow wide in panic, rare for him, and he rasps, "I can't breathe!" The more the nurse and the monitors reassure me that his respiration is normal the more frantically he insists, finally working himself into an asthma attack that subsides only when the nurse injects him with a sedative. He sleeps, throws up, and finally comes home with us at the darkest hour before dawn. I wake at five thirty to give a workshop to a middle school forty minutes away. It makes no sense, but there's no one to call, no way to cancel, and Matt, well sedated, is expected to sleep through the morning. His prognosis is good, and besides, Jeff is with him. Still, I slip out of the house aching, then driving in a numb haze. My audience nods knowingly as I use the story to punctuate the unpredictability of adolescent life. They seem to appreciate my workshop and offer to skip their break so that I can get back home by noon. Kindness waits only to be asked. I return to Matt, still sleeping soundly.

Truth be known: I believe in signs. But what are these signs telling me? That we should have stayed in New Hampshire? Well, bad things can happen there too. That we've got to be more careful about glass? Certainly. I've had all our storm doors changed to Plexiglas. Or can we take from all this a reminder to reach out to our neighbors as was the mode in New Hampshire, where neighborly interdependence is such the way of life – of survival sometimes when blizzards blow. "Flatlanders" as our friends up north might call us, are far more independent and, in turn, can seem more emotionally isolated, at least until an emergency arises. Our friends and neighbors at Loomis Chaffee have rallied around us this week as swiftly and surely as Joanne and Norm did at the moment of our greatest need. Matt will recover. God please let that be the big one and help us to take from it a sense of connectedness. Let us work to bring what we shared with our rural New Hampshire neighbors, to our community here in suburban Connecticut, our home.

The signs for Tim shine more clearly. When I take him to orientation at Watkinson School, I run into the new assistant head, Mike, on my way out. His five-year-old catches my attention. She wears a bright purple sweatshirt with an intimately familiar logo on it. It shows the silhouette sketch of children pulling a toy train atop the name "The Children's Meetinghouse." With the help of an artistic parent I designed that logo and chose that name for the pre-nursery school I founded twelve years ago when we lived at the Middlesex School in Concord, Massachusetts. My how it has grown – my third-born. Mike tells me that it now occupies the entire building across the road from the school and serves hundreds of children annually. Strangely, my grandmother was born and raised in that house as a Middlesex faculty child ninety years ago. If that's not enough to make me feel connected to Watkinson, Tim bops to school happily, an opening-day first, convinced that the Belgian waffles – his favorite – served in the dining hall at Loomis this morning, were a positive sign.

Suddenly, Di is gone. I feel the loss more profoundly and more personally than I could have possibly predicted: partly because it is so unexpected. Princess Diana married just a month before I married and gave birth to each of her boys just months before I gave birth to mine. On each occasion her public triumphs matched my private pleasures. I felt we lived parallel lives. She skied and went to theme parks with her boys as I did with mine. She sought children with medical needs in war zones as I taught children with special needs in schools. She bucked the royal administration that diminished her ability to lead as I bucked school administrations that diminished my ability to teach. Yet she displayed all the style, charity, and maternal instinct, albeit at great cost to the Princess of Wales, that I only yearn to emulate. Her life was so much greater, harder and now utterly tragic. In the same week, Mother Theresa leaves our world too, as gently as she lived in it. How fortunate I feel to have lived in the time of a truly saintly woman, making her wise words so real and so elusive:

Spread love everywhere you go: First of all in your own house. Give love to your children, to your wife or husband, to a next door neighbor ... Let no one ever come to you without leaving better and happier. Be the living expression of God's kindness: kindness in your face, kindness in your eyes, kindness in your smile, kindness in your warm greeting.

- Mother Theresa

We live on Loomis's "Faculty Row" where our backyard adjoins endless meadows. Flooded each spring by the confluence of the Farmington and Connecticut Rivers just beyond my sight, our meadows shine lush green in the fall with bushes bent by deer passing in the night and a choral whir of crickets broken occasionally by crow caws and far off commuter train whistles. Brittany grazes, sniffing for raccoons and skunks and the curious red fox, Five-o'clock Charlie, who hasn't made his usual dinner time appearance yet this year. In the hum of our now busy lives, I'm glad Brittany will keep me coming out here each morning to greet God and the day. Otherwise, I may forget that the goodness and peace nature offers is here as well as in the White Mountains. I just have to look harder here and make the time. It restores me. Restoration is going to be key, since I am making a career of restoring others: my students when they struggle academically, my student teachers when they don't know how to begin, and my children as they meet new challenges at new schools.

Matt's off and running: no surprise. He has been eager to attend Loomis since early childhood. While he attends his first class, I walk through Founders' Hall, where I used to teach philosophy. I slink like a voyeur, stealing through quiet halls that crescendo with the melodious murmur of teachers inviting students to study. Each displays his or her own style. Some foxtrot along a snowy blackboard; others waltz among their charges. I feel no envy, no regret from leaving that work. At ease in a backstage role now, the high-hope energy of the first day of school still washes over me like rain on a perfect, roll-up-your-pants and get-your-feet-wet day. School is home for Matt. What I hope most for him is plenty of challenges. He'll meet them.

Tim tells me the first day of school was tough. His computer teacher had the students read in turn from a computer manual. Faced with lots of unfamiliar words, Tim grew anxious. He counted heads and figured out exactly which selection he would have to read. With some whispered coaching from another student whom he hardly knew, he prepared for his turn, prepared to avoid humiliation. Voila! He managed the first round without embarrassment. On the second round, however, the teacher intermittently read a few selections, so Tim rehearsed the wrong lines twice. When finally his turn, he was asked to read a long selection he had not previewed at all. He abruptly asked to go to the bathroom, and there he stayed until all of the reading was sure to be over. A bit brutal for the first day, but he survived. And he wakes remarkably cheery for his second day of school. He grows. And our year away, our bumbling efforts at homeschooling, have paid off.

The first object of any act of learning, over and beyond the pleasure it may give, is that it should serve us in the future. Learning should not only take us somewhere; it should allow us later to go further more easily.

- Ted Sizer

Tim leads a charmed life. One day he relates that when he met with his learning skills specialist, she gave him some brief assessments. At one point he responded, "Oh you mean tongue-tappers!" She couldn't believe that he has already been introduced to the relatively new, Auditory Discrimination in Depth phonics program, which she finds so effective with her students who struggle with reading and spelling. She can't wait to continue the program Mrs. Howe started this summer: the only program through which Tim has ever made real progress. I am elated. I never considered asking that they continue the rare program. I never imagined that he might stumble upon a tutor so trained. What a happy fluke!

I have one as well. I run up to introduce myself to the head of Learning Power with whom I will be sharing an office at Loomis, and before the end of our conversation, she asks for my resume so that she can refer students to me for what she calls educational therapy. I like that. With my background in counseling and special education, educational therapy certainly describes what I have to offer. I begin to explore the certification process. Thus begins my new career as an educational therapist.

A t lunch in the dining hall one day, the director of the theater describes the fall production, *Runaways*, to me. He notes a powerful moment in the play when a deaf runaway signs to the audience about how it feels to be an outsider among outsiders. I suggest that I could call my friend, Judi, a psychologist at the American School for the Deaf, to see if she would like to bring a busload of her students over to see the performance. The director of curriculum and dean sitting with us express their delight. We decide on a date for the signed performance, and I call Judi that night to help us to hire sign language interpreters. Done deal. Opportunities abound to make exclusive prep schools more inclusive communities. I feel called.

To that very end I provide educational therapy to four students at Loomis so far, and midterm grades haven't even come in to spark academic concerns. I work with one young man who stands invincible in spite of years of difficulty, struggling but always trying for more success. He gives me joy. I give him strategies. I'm eager, as well, to work with students from non-traditional backgrounds, often students of color, who may find prep school and its privileged culture daunting, so I offer to provide support to students on full scholarship pro bono, and take on a few more students. Helping to complete the picture, the Capitol Region Educational Council has hired me for another workshop. They raise my fee commensurate with my experience, making it worth the over-preparation I put in and the considerable stage fright I battle. I also feel proud of my student teachers at Saint Joseph College, and during their midterm evaluation meetings, I get to show them how much and to challenge them further.

I madly weed my garden, left unguarded during our year away, for tomorrow the head of grounds plans to take me to a nursery to select perennials and more roses. My decrepit back complains, sciatic pain shooting down my leg with each hearty pull, but I cannot seem to stop. It just keeps looking lovelier and lovelier. My choked and starving Potentillas are so grateful for their new space and a long drink. They pop and bob golden in the sun. Joanne cements her best-neighbor-of-all-time award by veritably begging me to thin out her Shasta daisies. I love daisies. And I love that when I garden on the weekend or late in the afternoon, Joanne and her cunning kitten usually find their way out to their garden as well. Again I enjoy that feeling of unspoken connection that makes every chore lighter and richer.

Jeff finds a moment to join me weeding as the pink-striated sky releases its golden orb into a line of shadowy trees. "Sky-blue pink" he murmurs. The sky reminds him of popsicles he got from the Good Humor man's truck when he was young. He rescues my sore back, and we finally reconnect through the roses after weeks of his busy, busy preseason football and opening days at school. Several neighbors pause on their way home to admire our roses and our commitment to gardening together; one bears brownies. We gorge ourselves, smiling at each other, content to be together again tonight as we so often were on sabbatical, and happy to have a home at last to sink our souls into and to share with our friends. Later in the evening, I write:

Rose Shy and Courting

My rose is shy and courts me
for decades on end.
It hides at the edge of my view,
Reluctant,
curling from glaring eyes.
It unfolds full, warm, sweet
but crowded with petals:
many roles.

It awaits my approach
and touches my nuzzling nose
with the rich bouquet of home,
once brought to me at work
through a snowstorm.
When it bends away in the wind,
I cup my hands around its face,
beaming in full view.

Then it opens, slowly,
inviting me to touch
its gentle body,
and inhale deeply,
Relaxing
each breath,
in its care.

Tim returns buoyant from three days on retreat with his new schoolmates completely free of homesickness. Perhaps because they went to New Hampshire and it is home now too. He then proceeds to compose a survival story while typing on his Emate and spell-checking it entirely independently. I brim with the bittersweet pride of a mother who knows her child doesn't need her as much anymore.

My garden still needs me plenty. I have a truckload of roses and perennials to plant, feed, and water. Half are already in, and I've got the day free to coddle the rest. Jeff edged half the border last night and will follow me around tonight, when we can talk of Matt. When he gets the splint removed from his sewn-up wrist, he can begin playing football with protection. He can't wait. Neither can Jeff. I bite my overprotective tongue, worried over a tender nerve and several crucial veins just recently reconnected. I guess I have to let both boys take control of their own lives now.

It looks like rain. Perfect timing, if I can get everything in the ground! Tim joins me this afternoon to dig holes for the dozen roses along the road. We work tirelessly, side by side, muddy and happy. "You gonna pay me?" He suggests. "Well you are protecting my back, and it's so much more fun together." I guess this is where my boys start taking care of me.

I've got most of our books and dishes unpacked, and I've mounted all my framed pictures of our sabbatical escapades as well as several gleeful pictures of the boys from their cherubic childhood days. One black and white taken by a student in a photography course captures a remarkably pensive and soulful Tim at three. It fascinates me. Knowing him so well, I see him looking a little pissed off or just wary.

Next to that picture hangs one in which he stands smiling in goggles, arm in arm with Matt on top of a Mountain in Sundance. Matt is so much taller and self-assured in his smart skiing outfit and name-brand goggles. He has discovered his style, relaxed with a nice touch of class, and has started to do all the family's laundry for a clothing allowance. I never will be a shopper, so I am glad to relinquish both chores. I should finish setting up our house, but again I am drawn to the garden, fueled by the notice of our passing neighbors and knowing that my work brings pleasure to others as much as it delights me.

OCTOBER

Crickets chirp and a cool breeze encircles my bare feet as I type, wakefully. Tim's best buddy, John, spent the night, and he and Tim called for me at two AM to help them capture a noisy and persistent grasshopper that found its way into the house but didn't find its voice until we were all tucked into bed. Now it has joined the chorus outside, but I am still too alert to drop back to sleep as the boys have, so easily, after a few perfunctory whispers and giggles. They dug the holes for eight more roses yesterday, and I want to go out and plant them, but I am not quite willing to risk slating myself as the campus kook by gardening before dawn. I am sure my neighbors are already leery, while envying how madly I've been digging the earth, trying to develop an ebullient English garden before the frost hits and my burgeoning career, hopefully, robs me of my present leisure.

When they wake up and find me splattered with soil, shaking out the roots of my roses, Tim and John run out and ask if they can dig holes again. For an hour they have a ball, digging and throwing sod at each other. This earns them some cash to buy their Halloween costumes. They plan to be twin, killer clowns, bloodstained and eerie, and they need rainbow wigs. So I ask Matt, whom we seldom see these days, because he spends most of his waking hours on campus with his boarding friends, if he wants to invite a few fellow students to go to the mall with us later. Brilliant. After my long muddy shower with a fingernail brush that doesn't get all of the dirt out from under my nails, we meet at the dining hall and squeeze into our minivan: two preteens, three lumbering teenage boys and one slim girl who brings out Matt's sweet smile.

At the mall, I resist the urge to shadow my estranged eldest son and whisk the younger brothers away with a promise to meet at Taco Bell in an hour. I catch a glimpse of Matt now and then, checking out black light posters with his friends or leaning over Kaitlyn's shoulder closely to look at funny cards. When we meet up again, Kaitlyn greets me warmly, "Thank you so much, Mrs. Ross. It feels so good to get off campus and do things we would do at home." As we walk toward the car, Matt catches up to me and puts his arm around my waist, happily. Perhaps he'll find he can blend his new school life with his home life, after all. Though he must navigate the added pressure of both parents working at his school.

Now the house is filled with the smell of apple pie baking. From a tree at his school, Tim collected enough apples to fill a crust, and I am eager to reward his efforts. Jeff returns from a tough football game, grateful for a sweet snack and our company. His weekend game days are so long, but he loves coaching, while we miss him. Pleasantly, he settles in at home for the next twenty-one hours, before the week starts again with his coaches' meeting Sunday evening. As we munch, Tim spontaneously drags out his backpack and checks his planner. He reads his writing: "Social studies - wright a jernll log explaning pre day about leap, English - figur out 3 ways to mack storys beter, Math - factor game, Scinens - arplane test." Despite the fact that the math and science assignments are not due until Tuesday, he dives into them. His school has only two or three classes a day, in ninety-minute blocks. "It's perfect for me," I heard him tell John, "I can focus on those subjects rather than rushing around." He knows himself well, and I doubt he's alone. Most middle schools work at an unnecessarily frenetic pace. I enjoy listening as he and Jeff discuss the factors of ninety-nine and whether it is an abundant, deficient, or perfect number and what the heck those terms mean anyway. I interject an example I know Tim will visualize after helping me in the garden: "One of my roses is abundant with blooms and one is deficient." He's got it.

As in our homeschooling days, comfortably behind us, Jeff handles the math, while I handle the language arts. We still have the patterns of parenting and partnering we developed over the past year; they just lie dormant as we spin off into predominantly separate careers. He stays up for Matt's eleven o'clock return. I can't. At one, I dream that Jeff is in another room, and I can only see him through a mirror in the hall between us, but when he catches my eye in the reflection, he smiles, and I am reassured. When I awake, he is not in bed and the light is on downstairs. Down in the living room, I kneel by the couch and rest my head on his chest, he wakes and murmurs, "…must have fallen asleep." He drops his hand, caressing my back and dozes on. Pinch me, I must be dreaming. In the course of one day, Matt put his arm around me in front of his friends, Tim did homework on a Saturday night, and Jeff and I shared a reaffirming moment, sliding home.

"ilove you." Matt types this on the page, reaching with warm biceps resting on my shoulders. I keep it in. An immediate and tangible example of the process we've shared on sabbatical and in composing this book. In his element at last, he grins and gloats over his first Loomis Chaffee football game in which he wrapped his arms (one carefully splinted and padded) around a prospective scorer and grappled him to the ground. Jeff, as one of his coaches, nods and smiles in amusement, then rushes off to dorm duty. An hour later I am snuggled under Jeff's Amish heritage quilt clinging to the sound of Matt's voice, lilting and earnest, lingering in the air after he has gone to bed. Precious time. In the morning he follows me to the dining hall for breakfast. Odd. Usually nothing can get him up before absolutely necessary. As I collect my pancakes and juice, he slips by swallowing a sudden "see ya!" and slides into a seat next to a lovely, blond student who brings out his shy guy grin, worth its cost in orthodontia. And thus he is whisked away to school life until late tonight when he will have to study for hours in his room. Glory, he is being challenged. A student who always got by just doing his homework, Matt is being introduced to the concept of really studying. Still, he barely tolerates listening, briefly, when I recommend study techniques: previewing the text, highlighting his own notes, setting up at least two study periods for each test, etc. I can counsel his friends, and they've told him it helps, but I am not their mother.

Meeting my fifth student, I see that he is not sure he wants an educational therapist, but his parents are. I hope I can win him over by giving him the tools to be as independent as he thinks he already is. Fortunately, his first grades have hit him as hard as Matt's hit him. I heard Matt last night telling his grandmother, "Yeah, I never had to study before, but I'm getting the hang of it." I'll say! Though he shrugged off my prodding to get him to study for his first French and math tests, the disappointing results led him to allow me to guide him a bit in science. He claims that the class experiments measuring the nitrate and phosphates in the pond have nothing to do with the chapter of ecosystems and niches, pollution and acid rain. When I ask him about the effects of pollution on nitrate levels and the resulting changes in what populations can inhabit a pond, he heads back upstairs to study some more, to look deeper for connections. Days later he comes home with an A on a very comprehensive test. That's my boy. I am glad that French and algebra two challenge him, and I am glad that he has had this success in science to encourage him to spend the time studying, even when his social life calls. It's worth the time. Notre Dame remains on his college wish list. Of course, he is too young to be thinking so specifically about college, but dreams serve a purpose. They guide our choices and keep life on an enriching course, regardless of its final destination.

Supervising student teachers for the graduate school at Saint Joseph College, I am most concerned about a young, single mother of three children from Hartford. She sacrificed a lot to become a teacher, and I want to support her in this last step toward her certification. But teaching simply demands more than she gives right now. She needs to know it, and I need to tell her. And I need to do so directly, with respect for her considerable talent, and with tact, knowing that my race and socioeconomic standing makes it unreasonably easy for me to expect more.

She has arrived at school late several times and usually leaves the minute the students get on the bus to rush home to her kids and then off to her paying job. It's too much. However, student teachers are expected to follow the schedule of any effective teacher, arriving at least one half hour before the students and staying through the afternoon to plan, correct, and confer. This one has missed two faculty meetings already, and last week she rushed into school an hour after classes began. She didn't even call: inexcusable. But with an asthmatic child at home she had to contact her doctor first. Last weekend her ex-boyfriend beat her up and next weekend she is getting married: too much. I don't know how she is going to make it, but her determination to achieve her dream and her winning affirmation of her students encourage me to take her under my wing. If I learned anything last year, I learned to slow down and let life unfold. She could use that lesson right now. Easy for me to say, I know.

On David Watkinson Day, Jeff and I enjoy an informative dash through Tim's classes. His teacher of a class on ancient civilizations leaves puzzle pieces in front of each pair of parents. Instinctively we begin before she instructs us, she remains silent when the bell rings to start class, so we continue with our chosen task.

"There aren't enough edge pieces."

"Does anyone have any blue edge pieces?"

"Here you go!"

"No way, I'm not sharing"

"We're going to beat you guys."

"Let's put all the edge pieces together over here."

Just as we start to overcome competitiveness, the teacher asks, "What processes have you used?" And we respond,

"Categorizing."

"Trial and error."

"Grouping."

"Right! These are the processes that archeologists use to learn about ancient civilizations. Some share and some compete, fitting together artifacts and ideas about what ancient Greece and Rome were like." Good lesson in thinking skills.

Next, we visit Tim's favorite English class ever, where his English teacher describes how having her students read and write creation myths reinforces the history curriculum while teaching essential English language skills. This, from the teacher who won Tim over on the second day of school. He was poised on the edge of defiance facing yet another potential embarrassment, so common in his school life, when she confided to him, "I may not be like any English teacher you've ever had before. I am interested in your ideas, not how you spell them." She was in. Needless to say, Tim's creation myth wows us, but it is his poem about the sapling that elicits tears:

The Sapling

This is how the sapling

Got a new home:

It left the old abusive home

Leaving some roots behind.

Now that It's in its new home,

We must care for it feed

It, and help it grow

And adjust to its new home.

I am how I am; is this not enough?

Is it so wrong?

I'm rough and tough

Weak I'm strong

I'm smart and a fool;

I am my own person; I sing my own song.

Do you not like me; am I not cool?

Why do you want it to be like this?

We can just be friends;

We don't have to kiss.

I am who I am.

I like many sports:

Football, soccer, baseball, lacrosse, even bowling;

This is what I do, I and my cohorts.

We can be friends if you get the ball rolling

I am who I am; don't try to change me.

Timothy Wilson Ross

Each in their own way, my children are drawn to writing, to self-expression. I am so glad. They've so much to express: their thoughts, their passions, and even their pain. In any case, Tim's off to a good start in school. He scoffs that when he read his creation story in class, the boy sitting next to him, who had seen his flawed handwriting and spelling, insisted, "You just made that up. You didn't write that!" Tim tells me proudly, "I read exactly what I wrote. So I told him, 'I know, my spelling stinks, but I sure can write!'" My boy; my joy.

Either I'm a mother, or I'm a fool. On a Saturday afternoon, distorted bass drums pound and shrill voices scream through my head, followed in turn, by extraordinary expletives not worth repeating. For his fourteenth birthday, all Matt wanted was to experience the heavily advertised concert "The Radio 104 Big Day Off." I responded protectively, "Not without me!" If ever I wished I could retrieve my words from the air! I could not, so here I sit, more aware than my young teen of the soft scent of Patchouli failing to cover the smell of pot and clinging to black tee shirts that float by on wasted teenagers. I lean in to shout in Matt's ear, "I know that smell." He doesn't. "Keep it that way, and keep in mind that I know exactly what it smells like!" He chuckles, good-naturedly, "Don't worry." I will always worry, not out of a lack of trust in my young athlete and purist, but out of realism and awareness of his environment. The stinging smell of two skinheads peeing behind us blends with the voice of a band member asking two fans to stop making love (not the term he uses) in the crowd. I am glad that I came, glad that Matt experiences this mob mentality for the first time with my sobering influence close at hand. Finally, a decent group of musicians, MxPx, plays louder and harder but less vulgar rock as the "mosh pit" grows in size, frenzy, and hazard. Bodies slam-dance furiously, one or two occasionally lifted to surf the crowd. I am distinctly reminded and touch Matt's wrist. His hooked scar reminds us both that accidents happen too easily. "Don't ever mosh," I beg. He nods in stolid agreement. He looks rather bored and as unimpressed as I. "We'll be ready to leave soon," he assures me.

O
n Sunday I administer the Scholastic Aptitude Test to students whose learning disorders require that they be given extra time to ensure an accurate accounting of their abilities. Research has shown that this accommodation does not significantly improve the scores of students without impairments while significantly improving the scores of students with learning disabilities, fine motor problems, or attention deficits. Therefore, I am amused by the common concern that any parents would seek this accommodation for their more typically-abled children. Fortunately, the Educational Testing Service provides strict guidelines for students whose disabilities make them eligible for nonstandard administration of the SAT. The students respond well to my instructions and work quietly on their tests. One student who struggles with visual tracking and sequences answers every question directly in the test booklet and then has the time to transfer her responses to the answer sheet at the end of each section. Thus, she avoids her tendency to fall out of sync without realizing it. Another, so bright but burdened with word retrieval problems, works slowly and steadily, pausing pensively every so often to calmly recall the answer he requires. A third, hyperactive and distractible, takes a break to move around between subtests, clearing his mind and refocusing his attention. Given

that the same part of the brain controls attention as well as balance, the advantages of allowing a student with an attention deficit opportunities for extra movement seems self-explanatory. Such different, capable, intelligent students, it would be a shameful waste of talent if colleges couldn't see the extent of their innate abilities. However, it might be just as well to scrap such testing procedures altogether, as they were originally designed to favor white males, and still favor those who can afford the time and cost of test preparation courses.

My gifted but shaky student teacher is coming around. She has been on time or early for school every day since we talked. Planning more and winging it less, she has grown far more attentive to students' metacognitive processes. She thoughtfully teaches them to self-assess what areas they need to develop and to judge their own progress as well as she teaches her strong content. She has a great talent for teaching. At the beginning of her latest lesson, she has one math student write in a journal about how she struggled with regrouping the day before, a good self-assessment. Then they share a dynamic lesson during which the student shops through the L.L. Bean catalog for winter clothes. At the end, she writes about how much money she saved by calculating properly. I want to see more teaching of such self-awareness and intrinsic motivation in schools. It seems that stickers and popcorn only go so far to motivate kids. What really motivates even the most emotionally distraught children is awareness of their educational needs and daily success in meeting them. I am delighted that this student teacher has the key to authentic education, and I am eager to help her meet her goals.

Most of the Loomis Chaffee faculty seems to have mastered the patient practice of creating authentic learning moments. Daily, Matt is expected to assess his needs independently and to review past assignments and quizzes to determine what to study for his next evaluation. Growing more self-aware, he is much more forthcoming about his work with us. He now seems to appreciate our guidance, allowing me to suggest study skills and discussing courses with his dad. His work in science has been consistently excellent; he has such an affinity and aptitude for scientific observation. He has settled into his English and French courses as well, and advanced algebra, appropriately, keeps him hopping. Knowing where his hurdles lie, he clears them well. He likes that. My child who used to complete assignments at a minimal level and receive A's just for getting them in, now earns them and self-respect to boot. Diligent and demanding of himself, he fills me with great hope.

My students show great promise too. Academically, Bill found last year uncomfortable and disappointing. Yet, he is the consummate learner, curious and diligent, with deficits to overcome. I begin to write a comment for his parents, encapsulating our work together thus far:

> Bill has met some unexpected challenges with aplomb this fall. He made excellent use of his teacher's comments on his first history paper to improve his analysis of information in that course. On other papers, he worked to hone his thesis and to link each of his topic sentences as supporting structure. By replacing 'is' or 'said' with vivid verbs, he has

learned to thread his thesis throughout an essay and to enliven his writing. His reading speed waned over the summer, but he quickly used phrase reading to climb back from 190 words per minute to 250 words per minute with improved comprehension.

Preparing for tests, he made good use of highlighting to focus on key information in philosophy and to prioritize key information and formulas in physics. He has developed good self-advocacy skills. When frustrated because he was unsure of a teacher's expectations, he consulted with his advisor and addressed his questions directly and effectively with the teacher. He also asked to use his Emate for essay tests, which helped him to compose and spell more effectively. This winter, we hope to continue working on papers and to work on some Orton Gillingham syllabication strategies to improve Bill's spelling and reading.

Sincerely yours,

Mrs. Ross

I reread the comment. I like it; it summarizes most of our work together and alludes to the marvelous working relationship we have developed, so important for a kid so far from home and in the company of other kids for whom schoolwork comes so easily.

A t Exeter for the weekend, I find my mother's house, as ever, warm but not heated, clean but not tidy. It hollers, "Welcome; be one with us!" Though she and dad aren't home at the moment, the smell of her sweet, cinnamony applesauce lingers in the air and a note calls my attention to chicken and rice in the fridge next to a fresh bottle of my favorite wine. The clock ticks loudly, reminding me that she and Dad won't be back from Marta and Doug's until tomorrow. I sip and sink into Mum's cushy blue chair.

Friends from the UNH summer program join me for wine, and we head out to Applecrest, for cider donuts, apples, and maple syrup. We talk of John Irving's Cider House Rules and of growing up in apple orchard country. The drive along Hampton Road blooms with majestic maples chilled to a deep crimson and starting to shed. Peak has passed for the annual onslaught of leaf-peepers. Only the lowest leaves of golden birches remain green. Stately elder trees have bald branches spiking out on top like craggy, spindly fingers pointing recriminations at the cold, blue sky. Hot cider and warm smiles amongst the crowd at Applecrest complete my vision of the perfect fall day in New Hampshire.

At the UNH writers' reunion conference Don Murray walks us through his writing process. It's messy: a hodgepodge of random thoughts and images through which he sifts to find "the line." I so want to find the line for my reader. The line is the perfect moment or image described through diction, that is so personal and particular that it strikes a universal chord and calls to be written. Murray heeds the call. Characteristically self-effacing, he tells a story of how his colleagues offered him champagne one day. He was reluctant because he had three editorials to write. "Why? What are we celebrating?" Dumbfounded, his colleagues informed him that he had just won the Pulitzer Prize. He felt numb and detached for the rest of the afternoon, watching his coworkers celebrate his success. And all he could think about was that he not only had three editorials to write, but now they had to be written by a Pulitzer Prize winner! Only Murray, a jolly old elf sporting rainbow suspenders and sweet wife named Minnie Mae, could be so matter-of-fact, so unassuming, and so coy.

Donald Graves is a kind and gentle man who tells kind and gentle stories. After reading to a small group of us his story of a bus driver who extends himself to all of his passengers, he chats with me at length about my book. "How brave!" He commiserates when I tell him that I left chapter one on my dad's desk yesterday. "Yes, but how fortunate too. Now I know that the manuscript I send off to the world will be grammatically immaculate." I wonder aloud whether I should approach my work more like my father would: systematically researching and telling my family's story through the focus of definitive educational research. Graves narrows his eyes and touches my arm. "Just tell it." And so, I will.

Back home, I stroll through the yard sipping chamomile tea, a vehicle for sugar and heat. My five new dormant Simplicity rose bushes drink from the hose. I can't wait to see them in the spring, curling around the charming, gray split-rail fence alongside my house. By then I hope to have two summers' worth of weeds pulled out and replaced by random crowds of impudent impatiens, tall tulips, and dancing daffodils. I can't wait to see how the consulting practice I'm cultivating grows as well. Already I love attending to its variety of blooms: my activist workshops on disabilities and inclusion, my keen students, and my novice teachers. I enjoy the color and form each adds to my life and wonder which will need to be pruned back in the spring. I love my newfound independence at work and the opportunity to empower students and teachers in intimate and tangible ways.

Fall is the season for nurturing dormant hopes. Jeff hopes to begin coaching Loomis's varsity baseball team in the spring and to extend his expertise in his favorite arena. Matt hopes to heal well enough to catch for Jeff's team and then to play summer AAU. He also is determined to show us that he can meet any intellectual challenge that Loomis can offer – to our delight. Tim hopes finally to conquer reading completely and then to enjoy learning with fewer impediments. He also cradles his new lacrosse stick endlessly, the beginning of a new dream for which he shows great promise. He is so fast, fearless, and coordinated. And I carefully file away a letter from Bill's father that so aptly reflects my passion for educational therapy, my calling.

Dear Ms. Cole Ross:

I hope you and your family had a good holiday. I wanted to drop you a short note to say that I very much appreciate your work with Bill. His grades came in the mail… and I can't tell you how pleased I am with both the grades and importantly, the teachers' comments. In fact, your comments were particularly helpful in giving me a sense of how you are working with Bill … I know that Bill worked hard and these grades reflect that effort. At the same time however, he had a lot of wonderfully thoughtful support and for that I want to thank you. Somehow you and Bill really clicked this year. Possibly it is your experience in working with children who have dyslexia. It is really wonderful to see him gain confidence in his own ability as he begins to realize some academic success.

Again, thank you and our very best to you and your family in the New Year.

Best Regards,

Sincerely,

Mark

At sunset, my mums burst and the trees along the river match their hues of magenta and maize. Over a haze of city lights the sun sets, and I soak in the warm streaks of light breaking through the clouds. I have always thought that sun rays were a sign of God: probably an image from one of my favorite classic movies. Britty chases our neighborhood squirrel up my favorite copper maple tree. I missed that squirrel while we traveled. Tim named him Chester. I'll have to leave some nuts out for him to forage. I always assumed I would discover a new home for our family in New Hampshire. I guess I did. But it waited back in Connecticut all along: just longing to be noticed.

My garden glints at me this morning through a sugar coating of frost. Red and gold blossoms curl up, tinged with black. I rush to mound mulch around shivering roses, tucking them in for the long rest until spring. Then baseball will fill our lives again, centering this family as skiing does when it snows. The chill chides me to turn my energies inside our home: to sponge-paint the boys' bathroom in forest green and teal just like the Rainforest Café, the boy's favorite restaurant from our cross country travels; to find my elusive blue and white stoneware for semi-weekly family dinners, and to locate the remote control, lost for a week now and barely missed. I think I'll have a half-cord of wood delivered to bind us cozily around the fire and to remind us of our life in the hills. There, we desperately depended on woodstove heat. Here, we simply relish the gracious warmth and light that brings us together at the end of the day. Thus, I leave third base with these men of mine, leg extended, hitting the dirt on one hip, feet to the fire, sliding…safe…at home.

Five Years Later

2002

For years I have been shy about releasing my book for publication, but like mountains in the distance, looking back, the point of our story is clearer to me now. Though the book leaves off at an optimistic time, I am not convinced that the private schools we found for our children were the perfect answer. They were good matches, as I hope the boys' colleges will be, but we still had to poke and prod the boys and their teachers to make the most of their time together. In retrospect I don't feel compelled to tout homeschooling, public schooling, or private schooling. Each has brought our children great gifts and instructional disappointments. Class size is certainly key. What two teachers can accomplish with two students, free to take turns and to share our own passions, just cannot compare to a one to twenty-five teacher-student ratio. And the individualized instruction that the boys received in high school classes that always had fewer than fifteen students served them well. What I can tout definitively is parent involvement. An involvement that any one of my children's teachers could tell you, I have taken too far at times. But what is the saying? "You never know what's enough, until it's too much." Jeff and I have fought hard, though always with compassion, to get teachers to understand our kids as people and to provide for their unique learning needs. Our year of homeschooling helped us to know Matt and Tim better as learners, to recognize their struggles and their passions, and to pass on that knowledge.

Hopefully it also helped them to take charge of their own educations and to be good consumers in school. At times their self-awareness has led them to be impatient and cross with overburdened teachers. More times, it has led them to be strong self-advocates. I wonder at how much strife Tim has suffered, and caused, in his quest for meaningful learning that doesn't involve embarrassment. This boy who rolled his eyes in history class, only to come home each day and turn on the history channel. This boy who skipped physics class, only to get up early on Saturdays to note the calculations used to increase a car's performance on Spike TV. I wonder at Matt, who finally at age twenty, asked his college to assess his learning issues, then changed schools and took on strategies to deal with his attention deficit, so long obscured by his intelligence. These young men blaze Frost's "roads not taken" and make us shine with pride.

Our year in the mountains instilled something more prescient: an appreciation for nature, for family, for peace. Perhaps the essay Matt wrote last year illustrates this appreciation best while also demonstrating what a strong writer he has become:

The Lake

The ancient dirt road descends, shaded, and sheltered by the tall pine forest that stands above it, past Governor Wentworth's mansion, the icon of America's first summer resort in spite of being reduced to an old foundation. At night deer appear out of the cover of the forest, caught for an instant in the beam of your headlights only to return to the forest once again. You sit in the back of the minivan and stare, mouth agape at the nature that you have found yourself amidst after three hours of highway driving.

The road twists and bends downhill until it comes to the dirt pedestal that is the driveway, a rare, flat area supported by walls of logs on the downhill side that you chop at with your hatchet, amazed at your own strength and power. You park on and sprint off the platform, then down the small path with the smooth, embedded stone that your father has told you was carved by glaciers and scooped out of the valleys of the White Mountains thousands of years before you. You continue to run down the hill, over the rocks and onto the dock that goes clomp, clomp, shaking and shimmying with every step, and reaches out into the glacial crater that is now a lake, the lake, your lake.

You sit on the edge of the dock, your toes grazing the surface of the water made a mirrory black by the clear night. The sky above is huge and full of stars unobscured by smog or city lighting. The stars cannot be counted, but they appear so close that perhaps when you grew a little older, a little bigger, you could touch them. In the morning the sun will lift the shroud of darkness off the horizon and reveal the Belknap Mountains, a range of mountains created when North America crashed into Europe to create Pangaea. From your perch you can hear the loons wailing, the fish jumping, the frogs leaping in the water, and the chipmunks scurrying in the forest behind you. Amidst the noise that sounds like silence, you think about tomorrow, the wiffleball you will play, the corn you will husk, the barbecue chicken you will eat off the Fiestaware plates, the arrows you will shoot, the fish you will catch, and, if you're lucky, the ice cream you will go get at Bailey's downtown: cookies and cream with penuche sauce and whipped cream.

It begins to rain and you go into the old house, not fast like you were at home, but slowly, enjoying each drop. A fire is waiting, and you sit down to play Sorry with your family, making sure to use each Sorry card on your brother. The Red Sox game plays from the radio in the background, Joe Castiglione's Boston accent filling the room. Soon the hour is late, and you crawl up to your bed on the second floor, beneath the picture of the man fishing with the word "Quebec" written along the top. Listening to the rain fall on the frame roof and your brother breathing lightly to your left, you drift off to sleep, visions of homeruns, foot-long fish, and three scoop sundaes singing you to sleep.

- Matthew Brooks Ross

Ever the history teacher, Jeff asks me: what is my thesis, who is my audience, "So what?" So parents and teachers take heart: there is no ideal setting for learning, just as there is no ready-made home. It's all what you make of what's available. Capitalize on your privileges and circumvent your obstacles. Know your learner as well as you can, certainly remediate weaknesses, but put joy at the center of the experience, by accentuating, fostering, and celebrating his strengths. In the words of my dear mentor, Dr. Ned Hallowell, author of *The Childhood Roots of Adult Happiness* (2002),

Lead children to fall in love, to find passions to carry them through their lives with purpose and promise. Read them. Encourage them to connect with a mentor, to play with ideas and activities, to practice with diligence, to achieve mastery worth sharing, and to seek recognition, fostering more connection in an ever-expanding cycle of fulfillment.

Today Matt and Tim return, jubilant, from a day of skiing in New Hampshire. We gave Matt skis as a Christmas present and smiled when he chose to take his brother, among his closest friends, north to the mountains. He seems to get more attached to all of us the closer he gets to departing for college. We enjoyed another week with family in Ohio and New Hampshire recently, and though I know they won't be our last trips as a foursome, I also know that our trips together in the future will be more and more like chance reunions. And oh, what a union! I smile thinking how flawed and fortunate this family is and how much we appreciate each other's spirits and talents. I know we owe much of our closeness to our year away together, for truly,

Certain gestures made in childhood seem to have eternal repercussions.

— Anais Nin

We're so proud as Matt heads off to another year of college, bent on writing for the paper and catching for the varsity baseball team at Trinity this spring. Trinity offers fabulous English and history departments, and at the moment he hopes someday to serve his passion as a sports journalist or administrator. I recall, years ago, sitting on the edge of his chair, wrapping my arm around his shoulder, and telling him that I thought the secret to a happy life is to recognize and use the gifts God gives us. Now he leaves to develop his talent for catching and his gift for discussing. Spoiled by his sweet company, I will miss him even though he is nearby.

Tim shines shyly at eighteen. He retains his joie de vivre, especially on the lacrosse field where he flips and soars in freestyle fashion to make goals on his opponents, constantly caught unaware. They call him "the scoring machine." But his ability to assemble things astonishes us most, and we just want to find ways to feed that passion. During his ninth-grade year, after viewing a photograph of an Adirondack chair I liked, he designed and created it for me from scratch, and I found it waiting in my kitchen after just two hours. Three years later, a Chevy S-10 and a Porsche with a new Corvette engine adorn our yard alongside a go-cart with a completely new welded frame including full suspension, an upgraded, gravity-fed motor, and fat, not to be missed wheels. Without a lesson or a book, he completely redesigned and rebuilt that vehicle, and since then, he has made greater strides with larger vehicles through an independent study with our local mechanic. With considerable prodding from you-know-who, Watkinson has encouraged his passions, granting the independent study for two years to complement its traditional liberal arts program. Similarly, at school he has found great success in studying geometry and utter passion in the ceramics studio, where he spends free periods designing and forming true replicas of tall, ancient Greek urns and aerodynamic sports cars the world must wait to see. His hands and heart fly when he sculpts with clay or metal, and he spends hours researching cars on the internet almost every day. Seeing himself as a budding automotive designer or shop owner, he has begun to build an education that will support his dreams. Next year he attends Pennsylvania College of Technology to pursue his BA in automotive management.

As Loomis Chaffee's head baseball coach and associate director of admissions, Jeff is flying as well. His job now centers roundly on helping students with special interests, such as artistic or athletic skills, to discover how they might share and develop those skills at our school. He guides them to do so once they arrive, particularly on the football and baseball fields. Spending so many hours of free time on the baseball field, grooming and developing it into a state-of-the-art arena, he takes some teasing from our colleagues. I now understand why our grass sometimes has to wait while he attends to his "Field of Dreams." It is the sanctuary where he works the earth and instills strength and goodness in young men. So like Ray Kinsella's wife, I am beginning to harbor more pride and less resentment when people comment on that kooky guy who is "always out on that damn field." For our twentieth anniversary I found him eight baseball diamond gifts to match the eight diamonds on the ring he bought me. In particular, it thrilled me to find him a framed photograph of Fenway at sunset when our Red Sox beat the Yankees in 1999. It adorns our living room, reminding us of another magical playoff game at sunset in New England, along with antique advertisements and gloves made a century ago at the Draper and Maynard Factory in our own home away from home – Plymouth, New Hampshire.

We have just bought a charming, early nineteenth century home in Plymouth that we are renting for now, but hope to inhabit soon. Jeff and I pour over plans to restore it to its original quaintness, while adding our favorite 21st century amenities. Its large, attached barn provides plenty of room for Tim's car projects and for a private apartment upstairs, a retreat where Matt might disappear to write or the boys can visit to enjoy the lakes region or to ski. Anticipating our own extended progeny, we work to create a homestead near my parents' lake cottage for generations to enjoy.

Meanwhile, here in Connecticut, my dreams receive enormous support, and I stand grateful. Matt reads my manuscript and composes its introduction, an invaluable addition to the text and his first shot at publication. Tim has built a table, a shed, and a trellis for my garden, now overflowing with roses and perennials coaxed along for several summers. Jeff, after taking me on a sweet, nostalgic getaway back to Plymouth, helps me create a new office in the front rooms of our house, while conferring on the needs of our students, and recently editing our story. The college has hired me to teach prospective secondary school teachers how to embrace the needs of students with mild disabilities, still my cause. Several former students, including Bill, email me now and then from college and beyond where they embark on surely successful careers. My educational therapy practice, my book, and my graduate students quickly fill the spaces left by the independent men in my life, and my garden grows.

My emptying nest now overflows with new students who struggle to know themselves better as learners and to discover their passions and talents as well as the strategies that will help them achieve their dreams. It fills with novice teachers who want to know more about individualized instruction and how they can help students with disabilities to embrace and use their extraordinary brains. And now it chirps again with the story of our extraordinary year away in the country, loving family, national pastimes, and learning at home. Reassured, or rather compelled, by family and fellow writers, I may yet let my journal fly from the nest, hoping that it too, will score, sliding home.

Epilogue

2020

The boys have grown, married, and begun their families now and a pandemic has driven us all home. Jeff and I have moved to New Hampshire at last where we live with our young golden retriever, Maisie, and two cats, Mookie and Snickers. We farm and cook, hike and swim as we did on sabbatical. Like so many others these Covid days, my oldest brother, Doug's kids, Nathan and Kim are considering homeschooling their children in a neighborhood pod. Going back to school is risky for their children this year and unnecessary if they can juggle working online and teaching at home. They would love to teach with more traditional methods, as we did, on our sabbatical, and restrict their children's online time to opportunities to maintain social connections and play.

Like my own sons and many young parents today, they are considering a move from the suburbs to the country. Furloughed for the moment, I have time to write again and to find you, my readers. Sorry it has taken so long, but there were always more kids to teach and more teachers to support in what Dr. Bob Brooks calls compassionate teaching. Compassion indeed seems so elusive these days, and I long to see more of it. I hope you see some here.

Reliving our homeschooling year in order to share it with you, I am startled by how relevant our focus on learning at home has suddenly become in America. Indeed, nearly every family is doing it on some level. Instinctively, Jeff and I allocated much of the boys' time to self-directed learning and to innovation projects, just as schools do now by design, preparing students for the modern workforce. I am so pleased to notice how our pedagogical focus ultimately led each of our boys to pursue their passions. Our creative Matt became a farm-to-table chef, something he observed that one year when I had the time to cook from scratch most days. Our inventive Tim has taken innovation to a professional level, fabricating Porsche race cars for speed, safety, and style. Perhaps his first creation was a raft he built from old sailboat parts during our year in the Lakes Region.

I have found my thesis at last. I hope this story might help readers feel less alone in the solitude and more confident in the struggles that every teacher and parent encounters at one time or another, but especially now, driven home. I am sure each will find great resources, as we did along the way. All will find unexpected resources in themselves. Like it or not, intend it or not, we teach children from home every day. How daunting, yet how lovely that in this moment so many parents and teachers are challenged to do so more intentionally, more compassionately, more mindfully, if only for a year. It is a gift our children will cherish and pass along for generations.

References

Angelo, Maya, *Wouldn't Take Nothing for My Journey Now*, Random
House: New York, 1993.

Canfield, Jack and Hanson, Mark Victor, *Chicken Soup for the Soul*,
Health Communications, Inc: Deerfield Beach, Florida, 1993.

Hallowell, Dr. Edward, *The Childhood Roots of Adult Happiness*,
Ballantine Books: New York, 2002.

Johnson, Dr. Spencer and Constance, *The One-Minute Teacher:*
How to Teach Others to Teach Themselves, William Morrow
and Company: New York, 1988.

Peck, Scott, *The Road Less Traveled 1996 Calendar*, Andrews and
McMeel: Kansas City, 1995.

Stoddard, Alexandra, *Book of Days*, William Morrow and Company,
Inc: New York, 1994.

West, Thomas, *In the Mind's Eye*, Prometheus Books: Buffalo, 1991.
Williams, Margery, *The Velveteen Rabbit*, Avon Books: New
York, 1975.

Wright, M. Joy, *Gifted and Learning Disabled: Double Jeopardy or a*
Winning Combination? Learning, March/April 1997.

Appendix:
Sabbatical Lessons, Literature, Media, and Field Trips

Field Trips:

The Polar Caves

Boston Museum of Science

The Christa McCullough Planetarium

The Science Center of New Hampshire

The Toledo Zoo

The Culinary Institute of America

Hyde Park and the Franklin D. Roosevelt Museum

The Vanderbilt Mansion

Youngstown Labor Museum

The Butler Institute of Art

The Pro Football Hall of Fame

The College Football Hall of Fame

Train Travel from Utah to Ohio

Salt Lake City

Glenwood Springs

Denver

The Rocky Mountains

Gettysburg, PA

Williamsburg, VA

Washington, DC

Philadelphia PA

Savannah, GA

The Epcot Center, Orlando, FL

Montreal, Canada

The Baseball Hall of Fame

Valley Forge

Educational Films, Shows and Discussions:

Gandhi

Evita

The Scarlet Pimpernel

Pride and Prejudice

Nutrition and the Environment

Mogul Madness

Agony and the Ecstasy

The Vietnam War

The Odyssey (audio tape)

Gettysburg

Bill Nye The Science Guy

Krats Kreatures

National Geographic

Wild America

Magazine subscriptions the boys shared:

Ranger Rick

National Wildlife

Skiing

Extreme Mogul

Writing Workshop Lessons:

Journal Writing

Field trip responses

Letters

Research projects

The 5-paragraph essay:

Introductions with a strong lead

Organized support with citations

Reflective conclusions

Geography Lessons:

Southwestern Canyons and the Rocky Mountains

The Continental Divide

The White Mountains

The Steel Belt of Ohio and Indiana

The Eastern Seaboard

History Topics:

Elections past and present

Argentina and Eva Peron

Michelangelo and the Italian Renaissance

The Old West and Doc Holiday, Bill Cody and Annie Oakley

America and the Vietnam War

Science Topics:

> Lizards
>
> New Hampshire Flora and Fauna
>
> Chemistry in Cooking
>
> Rocks and Minerals
>
> Pond Life

1996-1997 Sabbatical Reading List Matt (Grade 8) Selected:

> Crichton, Michael: *Congo, Eaters of the Dead, Lost World,*
> *Rising Sun, Sphere, The Terminal Man*
>
> Davis, Don & Carter, *Art, Mountain Biking*
>
> Dumas, Alexandre, *The Count of Monte Cristo*
>
> Grisham, John, *A Time to Kill*
>
> Bennett, Lee, Editor, *Extra Innings: Baseball Poems*
>
> Kadupski, Charlie, Editor, *The Official Athletic College Guide:*
> *Baseball*
>
> Knowles, John, *A Separate Peace*
>
> Lee, Harper, *To Kill a Mockingbird*
>
> Orwell, George: *Animal Farm, 1984*
>
> Salinger, J.D., *Catcher in the Rye*
>
> Steinbeck, John, *Of Mice and Men*
>
> Alexandre Dumas, *The Three Musketeers*

1996-1997 Sabbatical Reading List Tim (grade 5) Selected:

> Roald Dahl: *The Twits, James and the Giant Peach, Fantastic*
> *Mr. Fox, The B.F.G.*

Beard, D. C., *The American Boy's Handybook*

Cassidy, John, *Earthsearch: A Kids' Geography Museum in a Book*

Connell, Richard, *The Most Dangerous Game*

Fox, Susan, *Guide to Owning a Rat*

Irving, W., *The Legend of Sleepy Hollow*

Schwartz, Alvin, *More Scary Stories to Tell in the Dark*

Van Riper, Guernsey, *Babe Ruth: One of Baseball's Greatest*

1996-1997 Daily Sabbatical Assignments for Tim:

Cast A Spell phonics

Times Tables

PAWS typing

Cursive writing

Journal writing

Silent reading

Math:

Text: Glencoe's Mathematics Applications and Connections: Middle School Course One (Grade Level: Six)

Tools for Problem Solving

Decimals: Addition, Subtraction and Multiplication

Fractions: Addition, Subtraction and Multiplication

Investigations in Geometry: Angles, Polygons, Congruence and Similarity

Ratio, Proportion and Percent

Calculating Area and Volume

Integers: Addition, Subtraction, Multiplication

1996-1997 Sabbatical Daily Assignments for Matt:

English:

Grammar, Comma usage

Parts of Speech

Journal writing

Silent reading

Math:

Introduction to Algebra: Variables and Equations

French:

As assigned by his tutor, Catherine E. Harrison

Acknowledgements

I am so grateful to all our friends and family who, throughout the story, made our homeschool experience work so well for our needs at the time. In particular, I thank Catherine Harrison, who taught Matt French long distance, a base we could not cover. With a full heart I thank my dad, Donald B. Cole for setting the example as a dedicated teacher, successful author and precise historian, an example I only aspire to meet. As soon as I thought I had it right, he read the manuscript and painstakingly provided all the original edits. Always struggling in awkward efforts to keep pace with his long and easy stride, I would love to show him my little book, nestled on the shelf amongst all ten of his. I am grateful to my father-in-law, Harry Ross, an erudite educator, who read the book with a grandfather's appreciation and an editor's eye, making further suggestions and enriching the telling of the story. Friends Dr. Ned Hallowell and Dr. Bob Brooks who have inspired compassionate teaching for decades, encouraged me about my manuscript and helped me to get it into the right readers' hands. I am grateful to my friends Andrea Chapin and Karen Merriam who brought precision and expertise as they made the final edits, two decades apart. To Tom Holbrook and Kellsey Metzger at Piscataqua Press, who believed in my work and its relevance to parents and teachers, and designed and published this book so expertly.

I harbor special thanks to two marvelous artists. First, my dear cousin Dawn Chandler, who guided me in selecting my cover photo and font with her impeccable taste and sense of color and form. And warm thanks to photographer Bill Truslow who ensured that all my photographs would be as compelling in black-and-white as they were in color. With his brilliant photographic skills he created an author's photo that is a work of art I never envisioned, because that's his department, not mine.

I offer my deepest appreciation to my sons Matt and Tim, in particular, for offering to share our story with other families facing the need and the opportunity to learn together at home. Their sweet spirits gave the story life. Matt's critical perspective and close memory of our experience together made him an invaluable editor when he read the manuscript later, during college, and his fluid introduction invites the reader into our home and adds authority to the tale. But most of all I thank my husband, Jeff, for creating the whole experience with me, for editing the manuscript and for always giving me the faith, time and the space to write and to teach. None of this story happens without him.

Made in the USA
Monee, IL
26 September 2021